the
NECESSITY
of an
ENEMY

RON CARPENTER JR.

HOW THE BATTLE YOU FACE IS YOUR BEST OPPORTUNITY

the
NECESSITY
of an
ENEMY

WATERBROOK
PRESS

The Necessity of an Enemy
Published by WaterBrook Press
12265 Oracle Boulevard, Suite 200
Colorado Springs, Colorado 80921

ISBN 978-0-307-73028-2

Cover design by Kelly Howard

Published in the United States by WaterBrook Multnomah, an imprint of the Crown Publishing Group, a division of Random House Inc., New York.

WaterBrook and its deer colophon are registered trademarks of Random House Inc.

Library of Congress Cataloging-in-Publication Data

Printed in the United States of America

Special Sales

CONTENTS

PART 3: THE TARGET • 55

PART 4: THE ENEMY WITHIN • 71

PART 5: WEAPONS OF
MASS DESTRUCTION • 97

PART 8: THE SPOILS OF VICTORY • 183

INTRODUCTION

This book is not just about how to defeat your enemies and properly put into perspective the adversities you encounter in your life. More than that, I believe this book will be for you a message of hope.

I believe it will show you that God is not only causing you to triumph over adversity but quite possibly repositioning you for your greatest moment. You could be Zacchaeus, the tax collector who climbed the tree, hoping to see Jesus—but not really expecting anything. However, your misfortunes are positioning you to receive a remarkable blessing. Remember:

With God there is no pain without purpose.

As I write these words in the fall of 2011, our nation is in the midst of what is certainly the worst economic climate of my lifetime. The downturn of 2008 is still with us. The Bible says that where a man's treasure is, so is his heart (Matthew 6:21). If you reverse-engineer that scripture, you can understand why, after heavy financial losses, so many people over the last four years have become disheartened. As their treasures left them, so did their hearts.

Proverbs 13:12 says that "hope deferred makes the heart sick." When you keep trying to get a job and you fail, when you try to save your house but you lose it, when you desperately try to hang on to your business but the doors close, hopelessness sets in.

In this bleak economy my belief is that the largest issue is not the financial problem but the heart problem.

So how can you rise from the ashes and be ready for a better day?

God uses adversity for our advantage. I trust that this book will help you seize and attack life with renewed enthusiasm as you gain a better understanding of your enemies.

Stand firm—you *will* rise from the ashes of any adversity. A bigger and better day is coming.

WHO WAS THE FRIEND?

I want you to consider something that may surprise you.

If you had lived in Judea in the first century and were acquainted with Jesus and His ministry, who among His twelve disciples would you have said was a close friend? Which disciple was Jesus's enemy (not *the* Enemy, Satan, but a flesh-and-blood enemy)?

His friends are usually identified as Peter, James, John, and the other faithful disciples. The enemy? That seems a no-brainer—has to be Judas, the notorious betrayer, right?

Now, I warn you: I'm going to mess with your mind, because in a moment I want you to consider a principle of the Christian life that's often ignored.

But first, back to my questions about Jesus and His relationships. Let's look first at a familiar incident involving one of Jesus's "buddies," the fiery, foot-in-mouth Peter. One day Jesus and the disciples were having a discussion, and Peter got high-fives for saying that Jesus was "the Christ." But a little later, when Peter pulled Jesus aside and started criticizing the Lord for saying that He had to go to Jerusalem to suffer and die, Jesus got in Peter's face and said, "Get behind Me, Satan!" (Matthew 16:13–23.)

Whoa! What happened to the "nice" Jesus?

Now flash forward a few days to the Garden of Gethsemane, where Jesus is in agony about upcoming events. Judas shows up with a group of soldiers who intend to take Jesus prisoner. The betrayer steps forward, greets Jesus, and gives Him a kiss. Jesus (who of course knows what's up) responds, "Friend, why have you come?"

The kiss is the secret signal to the soldiers that "this is the guy," and they rush forward to grab Jesus. One of the disciples—yup, it's Peter—pulls his sword and takes a whack at the head of a servant of the high priest, slashing off the poor man's ear. Jesus will have none of it and, after telling His "friend" he has it all wrong and needs to sheath his sword, says, "Do you think that I cannot now pray to My Father, and He will provide Me with more than twelve legions of angels? How then could the Scriptures be fulfilled, that it must happen thus?" And later Jesus also says, "All this was done that the Scriptures of the prophets might be fulfilled" (Matthew 26:50–56).

Now, I ask you, taking into consideration these two incidents involving Peter and Judas, which man ultimately did the most to advance Jesus's mission on earth? Who did Jesus call "Satan"? Who did Jesus greet as "Friend"?

Here's the point. The message Jesus was trying to get across to Peter was something like this: "You do not have in mind the things of God. You are trying to keep Me from the cross. Right now you are an enemy." And later, Jesus effectively said to Judas, "You have come to sell Me out so that I will complete My destiny. You, therefore, are My friend."

In this circumstance—which because of the Cross is the most important moment in history—Judas did for Jesus what Peter and the other disciples could not do.

You already know that God's ways, including His view of enemies, are different from our ways. But an understanding of how God uses people coming against us and situations that are very negative can change everything.

If we are to make authentic progress in life, we have to face up to *the necessity of an enemy.*

THE WORST DAY...OR
THE BEST DAY?

Have you ever had a day when, by about noon, all you wanted to do was go home and crawl up in your mama's lap?

I know, grown men are probably not supposed to say things like that, but likely my worst "run to mama day" was September 24, 2007. Without that day I don't think I would ever have learned the life-altering message of this book.

On that fall day, there I was—a well-known pastor in the community of Greenville, South Carolina—sitting in a room with steel walls and no windows, sweat running down my sides, my head pounding like a drum as three FBI agents fired one question after another at me.

As you may have guessed, I wasn't in the federal building in Greenville that day to conduct any pastoral duties. No, I was under investigation for possible criminal activity. As the hours dragged on, all I could think was, *How did I end up here? Why is this happening to me?*

And the irony of my predicament was that it was my purpose in life and my calling to be a pastor that had gotten me into this mess!

Let me tell some of the backstory.

In 2002, our church in South Carolina was approached by a businessman from another state. He seemed to be a consummate professional and came highly recommended. He told us of a program he'd developed that would lead people who were down on their luck, particularly single moms, toward home ownership. This was a turnkey proposition, as this businessman had already prequalified and lined up home builders, financial institutions, and representatives from other legitimate companies so that an individual with few resources and bad credit could go through financial training and rehabilitation and become a first-time home buyer.

I loved the idea because helping people is why I'm breathing, and it always has been a huge emphasis in our church. Any day I can show people in need how God can help them realize their dreams and get on their feet—that's a very good day for me! In short order we got all over this idea.

But, having been in ministry for a while and knowing that talk is cheap, I insisted that we not go into this deal blind. So our team did our due diligence by conducting extensive, hands-on investigations into every aspect of the project. We ran credit checks on the businessman and even took the whole plan to the attorney general of South Carolina for review. He gave it a thumbs-up, so we enthusiastically kicked everything into gear.

About 250 people from our church got involved—almost all of them single moms. The early results were amazing! People began making sense of their finances and changing bad habits. My best friend and ministry partner—my wife, Hope—and I were like two kids locked in a candy store. We were thrilled and so grateful at what God was doing for single moms and their kids.

We should not have been so excited. What we didn't know was that our business partner was meeting secretly with wealthier members in our congregation, enticing them to invest in the project. Checks for thousands of dollars were flowing into our business "partner's" bank account.

After about ten months, when the businessman had accumulated over $1 million (most of it from our church members), he stopped returning phone calls. The next thing we knew, the money had disappeared and so had he. It was no comfort at all to find out later that the FBI was on his trail for similar fraud in another state.

All hell broke loose. After a phone call informing me of the crisis, I cut short a speaking engagement in San Francisco and flew home. Many people were very angry at me because I was their pastor—the one who had encouraged them to participate in the program. Call after call came asking me or the church to refund money. But I had never had that money, and neither I nor the church could do anything about it.

Media outlets had reporters, once my friends but now resembling enemies, pushing cameras in my face. Local talk-show hosts, who had previously applauded our community impact efforts, were now howling at us like ferocious animals. Police were stationed in my front yard because of threats to my family from people who had once called me Pastor. I was a prisoner in my own house, my wife was depressed, and my kids had to change schools to escape ridicule from former friends. Our life had taken a major turn that we'd never anticipated. The pressure became so intense on my family and ministry, I wondered if I'd ever survive.

Every track record of success that had been laid, everything about me, my heart, and my motives was in question. In a million years I never would have dreamed I would be in this situation.

How would you feel if your life had taken this turn?

I'm certainly not minimizing any trial you may be facing now, but I do want you to understand what I endured so you can recognize the power of the truth I'm about to share! It will change your paradigm of how you see people around you.

It was during this low point in my life that I felt I was surrounded by enemies, much like you may be feeling right now in your own battle in life. It was then I realized a truth firsthand (a principle I'll talk about more in depth later): the ultimate enemy of our souls is Satan, and I learned through my study of Scripture during my personal tragedy the truth about how he operates through people.

The Bible is clear: because we live in a natural world with natural authority established by God as unbreakable, people can be used by God to be the windows of heaven or by Satan to be the gates of hell.

That's how your real Enemy shows up, through people he uses as enemies. Enemies, therefore, aren't people who cut in front of you in the lunch line, or cut you off at the traffic light. They are people who have allowed Satan the opportunity to work through them, as the gates of hell into your life, to oppose your destiny and your purpose; they set their desires against what God has in line for your life.

In a matter of days, my successful, comfortable life as the pastor of a growing, effective church crumbled. I had done nothing wrong, but people were accusing me of misdeeds, trampling on my good name, and calling me foul names. I felt surrounded by enemies.

What in the world was happening to me?

———

What about you? Are you facing something—or *somebody*—in your life now that is causing you pain and stress that just won't go away? Maybe it's a banker who won't give you the loan, a best friend who's stabbed you in the back, or a family that no longer invites you to Thanksgiving? Are you baffled? confused? intimidated? threatened? heartbroken?

Maybe you have a plan or a dream that you know in your gut is your destiny, but something is standing in the way.

Enemies are the people, mind-sets, weaknesses, and situations in your life that try to destroy the passion you have for God's purpose and plans for you.

I have some important news for you: to fulfill your purpose and stay true to your calling, you'll need to understand the reason for enemies. If you do that, then when they rise up against you, you will quickly recognize what's happening.

The truth is, it's not really them—it's the ultimate enemy, Satan, who is using them to try to sabotage and abort your future.

As I was determining how to respond to the enemies coming against me from all sides, I found one scripture that I hung on to like a drowning man grasping a piece of wood: "Our light affliction, which is but for a moment, is working for us a far more exceeding and eternal weight of glory" (2 Corinthians 4:17).

What this means is that all our afflictions or problems in life, no matter how horrible they seem, are not a big deal compared to the payoff for facing and enduring them. And the results for us in heaven will be great and eternal.

You may not know me, but if you did, you would understand that I sometimes say things that have an edge to them. I grew up in a wide space in the road called Possum Kingdom, South Carolina. People there are known for saying what's on their minds in a blunt fashion. That's how I am as a pastor, and now I'm going to say something that may rattle you a bit:

You will never be an exceptional person if you fight only ordinary battles.

I had always prayed that God would use me exceptionally, let me stand out from the crowd, have me do things that had never been done before. But what I concluded, primarily after living through the story that is the basis for this book, was that I was going to have to fight battles I'd never fought before. And until this major crisis in my life, I had never put those two concepts together.

What I know now for sure is that we all need a really good enemy now and then. For example, in a sport like college football...

If you want to be No. 1, you can't just beat No. 9!

Honestly, the right fight can be a good thing in your life.

And if there are no enemies on your horizon, don't worry, they will show up in due time if you sincerely want to follow God in this world.

———

Ever since a guy named Job had a few problems, the question, *Why do bad things happen to good people?* has been on the lips of almost everyone alive. Having been directly impacted by this notion myself, I chose to write this book.

To be candid, I never had heard anyone (myself included) adequately explain why so much suffering can fall on a person who is just trying to live a godly life. Regardless of the type of pain each individual experiences, it's a universal question that usually goes like this: "I know I'm not perfect, but I am trying really hard to do the right things. So why is my world falling apart?"

Now it was my turn to ask the question.

Based on a profound personal crisis and some heavy lifting with the Word of God, this book is my attempt to deepen our understanding of the meaning of suffering.

The Bible's perspective on adversity is that it is always working for you. Sometimes God sends it. And even if He doesn't, He still uses it.

So, as a biblical believer, I conclude:

There is no way to lose in any given situation.

I believe if we understand why we might be going through something, the grace and strength to see it through will be there. But if we don't know why tough things have fallen in our laps, it's hard to stay focused.

That wisest of all men, Solomon, once said, "In all your getting, get understanding" (Proverbs 4:7).

I was in a situation where I desperately needed understanding. I had to have it!

It was day by day, God and me, tears on the floor, my Bible open, clawing my way out of a hole. And every day God gave me a revelation of thought, another piece to the puzzle, and in time I saw the picture of what I was going through. I was in the process of moving on to a greater day, like what Paul wrote: "For a great and effective door has opened to me, and there are many adversaries" (1 Corinthians 16:9).

I realized that there's a pattern to how God moves us along in life: right before you open a new door of opportunity, there's some giant you have to slay. And in my land of giants, I had to rise above my pain and open that door.

I saw the pattern, from Genesis to Revelation, revealed in the lives of men and women of the Bible as well as in what the Bible teaches. This inspired me to take action, to position myself for my future instead of wallowing in my pain and self-pity.

The arrival of an enemy in your life is a sign to you that this present season you're in is finally coming to an end. God often assigns an enemy as a catalyst for you to exit one season and enter another.

We might never have known anything about David if God had not arranged for Goliath to arise between David and his kingship. It's a compelling story—one day David was delivering cheese and biscuits and ended up killing a giant. The next day he was carried through downtown Jerusalem, with women hanging over balconies singing songs to his name. Would any of that have happened without a great enemy?

What would the nation Israel have been without Moses facing down Pharaoh before the great migration out of Egypt? Maybe those 450 years of slavery the Jews endured would have lasted much longer.

Even Jesus lived in anonymity until Satan determined that He was more than Joseph the carpenter's oldest boy.

Here's why I say an enemy is a necessity:

There's a Goliath, a Pharaoh, a Satan standing between you and who you are destined to become.

As you move through life and ascend to new levels of potential and breakthrough, you'll discover that your enemies are just as essential as your friends; in fact, they may be even more critical in your times of transition, if you'll recognize them for the stepstools they are for you.

Enemies are indicators to you that God is planning movement in your life, and transition is right around the corner.

I do want to make a couple of things clear: My intent here is not to turn you into an obsessive enemy hunter. The Bible teaches us to watch, not to search, for trouble. It can happen that the Enemy will use a demonic spirit to challenge your purpose and rob you of your potential, but I believe this is rare. The vast majority of the time, your enemy will show up in the form of a person, a mindset, a situation, or an internal struggle. The remainder of the book explains all of this.

And, I want to issue a particular heads-up to husbands and wives and moms and dads. The enemy is not your spouse or your child! Marriage and parenthood are examples of a covenant relationship. These are meant to go the distance in life. They are usually incredibly challenging relationships and require huge amounts of work.

I will give you this—there are times when it seems like a spouse or child is the enemy! But he or she is not. The enemy is the issue between you that may be driving you crazy! Our responsibility is to fight the problem, not the person.

—

As a result of my journey, I want you to know that if you are in crisis or feeling beaten down for any reason, life has not handed you something sour just because life doesn't like you. Life has handed you an opportunity to open a great door. But you need a correct perspective on your difficulty. This is how I like to describe it:

An enemy arising in your life is a key indicator that the next stage of your future is about to be born.

That's what this book is about. This is a perspective out of the Word of God that saved my life. I had to learn that an enemy can be a blessing, not a curse. I journeyed through the Bible to make sure that this principle is consistent throughout Scripture. I found that in the life of many great Bible heroes, it was a great enemy that catapulted each of them to a great place and multiplied their influence.

- It was Potiphar's wife, through her false accusations, who sent Joseph to prison and ultimately opened the door for him to become a prince (Genesis 39).
- It was Pharaoh whose persecution served to multiply the Israelites into a mighty nation (Exodus 1).
- It was also Pharaoh who, by multiplying the power and influence of Moses, forced this fugitive to become the historic leader of a mighty nation (Exodus 5–12).
- It was Delilah who caused Samson to renew his strength and multiply his influence by killing more Philistines in his second season than he did in his first (Judges 13–16).

- It was Goliath who took David from obscurity to notoriety, from sheepherder to king (1 Samuel 17–18).
- It was a shipwreck that enabled Paul to share the gospel with the inhabitants of an entire island (Acts 27–28).
- Even Jesus Himself had to fight the enemy of His own will in the Garden of Gethsemane (Luke 22:39–45) to receive a name above all names, that at His name every knee would bow and every tongue confess that He is Lord (Philippians 2:9–11).

I reached the lowest point of my life during this series of events, but when I knew for certain that I wasn't going through pain for the sake of pain, I found hope. I discovered I was going through pain for the sake of promotion.

There's something about facing life's enemies that enlarges your capacity. I'm not just talking about external challenges. I'm talking about internal changes that increase our ability to grow stronger, to have the "fuel" for future battles.

You can see what battles with enemies did for Joseph, Moses, Samson, David, Paul, and others. For me, by God's grace and mercy, this biblical principle fueled me to overcome great days of adversity and changed my perspective on life, family, ministry, and my future.

Overcoming these enemies creates such a great internal strength that you become like Joshua and Caleb who, after looking at the giants in the land, said in so many words, "Aw, they're just bread for us! We will eat these giants!" The other ten spies were scared, but Joshua and Caleb saw the giants that would become the fuel for power and strength (Numbers 14:9).

In my darkest day, when I felt I had no friends, I opened the Word of God and found *many* friends with many similarities. Then I understood why the Bible says we're "surrounded by so great a cloud of witnesses" (Hebrews 12:1).

I could hear the cheers of David, Joshua, Moses, and the others ringing in my ears: "Get up, Ron! Get up! This is not your worst day! This is God's greatest opportunity!"

That's why there's a necessity for an enemy.

PART 1

THE NECESSITY

The necessity of an enemy?

Necessity? Really? Should we really believe that great progress for God in life *requires* an enemy?

I do. But I understand why you would appreciate some explanation.

To be candid with you, until my crisis hit in 2004, I had experienced some adversity, but nothing quite like the fire-breathing enemy monster I met when my world fell apart.

When I speak of enemies in this book, I'm not talking about your basement flooding or hangnails or red lights that don't turn green fast enough! I'm also not talking about some habit you might have, like leaving your underpants on the bathroom floor. Those kinds of things are a part of life, and to one degree or another require attention, but they are not your enemies.

When I talk about enemies, I mean this: an enemy is any circumstance, any person, any deep-seated sin, any crippling character flaw—really anything the devil can dream up—that threatens the completion of God's purpose for your life.

I've received a lot of criticism for using the word *enemy*. "Isn't that a bit *extreme*?" No, it's not: if you don't see something that comes against God's purpose for your life as an enemy, you won't take the aggressive, proactive, even violent action against it that's required to conquer it before it conquers you.

I cannot tell you how many enemies of significant magnitude will come against you in your lifetime, but I'm confident that if you are a child of God, they will come. Someday you will see a Goliath marching toward you across the field, and you are going to have to fight, or that giant will eat your lunch.

Thankfully, if you have Jesus on your side, you have all the resources necessary to eat the Enemy's lunch! Get this:

> For though we walk in the flesh, we do not war according to the flesh. For the weapons of our warfare are not carnal but *mighty in God.* (2 Corinthians 10:3–4, emphasis added)

It doesn't matter how big your Goliath is. There is *nothing to fear*!

SINGING FOR SOME SHEEP

For many years I dealt with many adversities, but I always seemed to live not far from God's blessings. I got kicked in the face now and then but kept all my teeth. For the first fifteen years or so of our ministry, my wife, Hope, and I faced many challenges and struggled, but things always seemed to work out.

Even from early in our relationship, Hope and I had only wanted to help Jesus find, love, and heal His sheep. But sheep care isn't always pretty.

When we started the church, we had no money and no plan. We just knew God was calling us to the Greenville area to serve Him. We didn't have a clue about market trends; we just loved Jesus and cared about people. We knew the people of the world were lost, and we wanted to see all of them saved and their lives turned around. So wherever we went, we asked people if they had friends who didn't know Jesus or could benefit from a friendly church.

If we got a positive response, I'd whip out a napkin to scribble down a name, phone number, and address. Then I'd go home and call the person, and if the number was wrong, I'd try for an hour to hit every possible combination of the digits on the napkin, realizing some of the information came from less than sober sources to begin with!

I didn't care. I was on fire for God and had a lot of time on my hands. I had no idea that the Joes and Willies and Bubbas I was writing down on napkins were broke, busted, and disgusted. It didn't matter—they were sheep who needed a Shepherd, and I was going to round them up.

That's how I ended up embarking on a short-lived singing career.

One day I rolled up to a house where, supposedly, a talented musician and his wife lived. I was excited, thinking, *He could be my first praise team member!*

When I came up the sidewalk, I saw two massive speakers on the porch. I mean, they were as big as Volkswagens, both blasting out a Hank Williams Jr. song so loud that the air was vibrating. Sitting on a chair was a man (the musician?) wearing torn overalls and holding the longest shotgun I'd ever seen.

A woman was beside him (I assumed it was his wife), and she was cussing him out for his drinking. The lady sure had a colorful vocabulary! Always looking for the positive, my thoughts moved on from *potential praise team member* to *Ah, yes, my first domestic dispute! Help me, Jesus, bring some peace.* The man, who I could tell was drunk as a skunk, now had his shotgun pointed right at me. I discerned that he did not want me invading his personal space on that porch, even though all I wanted to do was bring him some love from Jesus.

His wife kept on screaming profanities, which wasn't helping matters, especially since she was cranking more amps than Hank Williams Jr.

I quickly surmised that this situation had not been covered in Bible school.

As my foot hit the first step, the man cocked the shotgun. Sizing me up through one squinty eye, he said with an inebriated growl, "Just who the hell are you? Whatcha want, boy?"

Now, I'm pretty quick on my feet, so I shouted, "Whoa, whoa! Don't shoot me. I'm a preacher!"

About then, the man's wife, who had moved indoors and was peeking through a curtain, began shouting, "He crazy! He crazy!" Charming little couple.

She snapped the curtains shut, and I was alone with my new friend. And his shotgun. And his thundering Hank Williams Jr. And what was left of his second bottle of whiskey.

"I'm a preacher. I jus' wanna invite you to church this Sunday, brother!" I yelled above Hank's song.

The man adjusted the aim of his shotgun, pointing it at parts of me I didn't enjoy thinking about losing. Then he yelled, "Sing, preacher!"

I instantly realized I had two choices: sing a country music lyric or become a country music lyric. So, as if taken over by the Holy Spirit Himself, I witnessed an amazing, uncontrollable thing: my hands shot straight up in the air, and I began belting out, "Awwwlll my rowdy friends are comin' over tonight!"

One thing's for sure: I never was so thankful that I knew some lyrics to songs by Hank Williams Jr. (And I know that reveals I wasn't always listening to praise music myself.)

My singing must have passed. I left that house in one piece.

Our church had modest beginnings. The first church building was a warehouse with no heat, no carpet, and no air conditioning. We hung some shower curtains on the concrete wall to cover up the loading-dock doors. Every penny was precious, so our stage was nothing but two-by-twelves flipped on their sides and covered with plywood, on which I preached using a nineteen-dollar RadioShack microphone. Our worship leader led the music using a donated upright piano that had no top and wouldn't stay in tune. We had forty rusting metal chairs.

I do not have one of those stories where I started a church and six months later a thousand people were pushing the walls out. No, Hope and I basically spent about three years without any salary attracting people who were in the same situation we were—broke and living on food stamps and other government assistance. We grew person by person, family by family.

There were plenty of challenges and some setbacks, but God always blessed us. And it didn't seem we had many enemies.

WHY ARE ENEMIES NECESSARY?

know you still may be thinking, "Is there really no other way for God to accomplish His goals for us except with this 'slay the giants' routine?"

A good question. Most of us who have been around church for a while are comfortable with a more benign scenario. Aren't Christians supposed to be nice, peaceable folks known for loving others and doing good deeds? Why would such people have enemies?

The big-picture answer is the war between the kingdom of God and all its enemies. Until Jesus comes back, we are all living behind enemy lines. The war may have been won, but skirmishes and even all-out battles are just the way it is.

But the more critical reason we have enemies is that your life and mine count for something. We are not accidents. You and I have a role to play in an epic drama that involves a God who has grand purposes.

God has intent about every person's life, which means no one was a mistake.

You may have been the product of an affair, a rape, even incest; but God chose to bring life through that experience, in the form of *you*. God was intentional with your arrival.

I've known since I was young that I was destined to be a preacher. So when my run-in with the FBI came about, I wondered, why after twenty-plus years of a growing ministry was I faced with losing it all? Had I messed up in some way? Had God left the building? What was He thinking?

I wasn't really ready to admit it, but what I had done for so long in ministry wasn't working that well anymore. I was a bit stuck. I needed to try some new things, and our church needed a fresh vision. But change is not easy. I wish it could have happened some other way, but I needed an enemy to blast me out of my comfort zone.

I needed to learn in a deeper way that God has a lot of plans for the world, plans that include you and me.

THE PURPOSE OF IT ALL

God has something unique planned for each of us to do. The Enemy doesn't like this.

Do you know what your purpose is? If you don't, as you'll learn throughout this book, it may be more difficult for you to determine what and who are the true enemies coming against you.

As I mentioned, I've known since I was young that I would be a pastor. And later, as we began the ministry in Greenville, I gained a clear understanding of the specifics—some mandates—of how that ministry was to look.

As I tell more of the story of my encounter with enemies, you will see—because I had a clear understanding of my purpose and the mandates on our church's ministry—why I knew I was in a serious fight and had to dig in. The Enemy—or rather, enemies, were coming against my purpose.

You and I have an enemy, Satan, who wants to ensure that the purposes of God are not accomplished. And he uses people and whatever else is available. So whenever I see something or someone that stands in the way of the mandates of God's purpose on my life, I identify them as enemies that I must engage. Ultimately, the battle will be the Lord's, and when it's over, these enemies will be my footstool. But I have to do the fighting.

So what do I mean by purpose? For many people it's a vague concept that doesn't have much useful meaning. That's unfortunate. I do not have nearly the space here to fully explain how anyone can find purpose, but this is a brief overview:

Based on a lot of good instruction from others and my own study and experience, basically I believe purpose relates to the fact that the Bible says our lives are "hidden with Christ in God" (Colossians 3:3). I believe God has planned your whole life in heaven. The Bible says He foreknew you, predestined you, called you, justified you, glorified you—and all of it is past tense. And He also wants what's in heaven to be done on earth.

Another way to understand this is to think in terms of how a frame defines a house. When you look at the evolution of a building project, you can understand that while the house's framework is part of the finished building, the framework itself is not the actual building.

If you walk by a new house under construction, you'll see the building crew working on the framing. At this point in its development, you can't tell many details about the house. Without reading the blueprints, there's no clue what the exterior walls will look like, if there will be brick or stone around the fireplace, or what type of countertop is going in the kitchen. And even the blueprint won't show you final details, like the style of furniture the owner will choose.

However, by looking at all those two-by-fours and two-by-sixes that make up the framework, you can see the general shape the house will take.

When God gives you an insight about your purpose, this is a framework being set in place within which the life that lies ahead of you will be lived. You don't know all the details and everything in every moment that will take place, but you can see, as construction continues, the framework of what the Architect intends.

When I was a young man, I knew God had given me an insight that someday I would be in ministry. I had few details of what price tag would hang on that framework. I certainly knew nothing of the battles I would face and the giants I would have to slay. However, having this sketch of my future in ministry gave me an understanding of how I would be spending my time and, consequently, how I would not be spending my time. It gave me a framework for my daily activities, as opposed to how my day might look in a different calling.

So I believe you arrive at your purpose through a number of things, such as through a devotional life and through people God assigns with oversight in your life—individuals who see things in you that you don't see. Purpose has many clues and many indicators—it won't just be God taking you on the side of a mountain like He did with Moses. It's you seeing the pieces of your life and answering questions such as, Why do I think like I think? Why am I tied to who I'm tied to? Why have specific voices been placed in my life? What do I value? What is my specific set of gifts?

Your gifts are clues and indicators as to what you've been put on the earth to do.

God also positions you in certain places, even certain geographical locations. And once all these indicators and clues are assembled, you begin to snap together pieces to the puzzle, which in time starts looking like a picture.

And all that together begins to clarify your purpose, so you conclude, *Well, this must be why I'm on the earth.* Then you begin to pursue that picture as God opens doors and orders your steps. And the reality is that as you move closer and closer to completing that picture, there are many doors you have to open and many enemies you have to slay along the way.

By the way, I don't believe God gets involved in every single little struggle of my life. He doesn't get His nerves shot when my kid gets called to the principal's office or my printer runs out of ink.

Some people want God to get "tore up" every time they get "tore up." Of course He cares about the details of our lives, but I think He only gets "tore up" when a battle threatens our purpose, because He has already ordered our steps toward an intended end.

Solomon wrote in Ecclesiastes 3 that life will take you through seasons; there's a time to live and a time to die, a time to mourn and a time to rejoice, and so on. I believe enemies will come along to show you these seasonal changes. It is those adversities in life that you have to conquer when they pop up. They are signifying to you that one thing is finished and another thing is beginning—that you are heading toward full completion of the purpose God has assigned you.

—

I want to finish the story of the man who gave me a new appreciation for my interest in country music.

I was a little surprised when, three weeks later, that guy with the 12-gauge became the third member of our church—and our first praise team drummer! Granted, it took awhile for him to overcome his drinking problem. So each Sunday morning I'd come to church early, brew a pot of strong coffee, and pour the joe down his throat to sober him up in time to play drums for worship.

I'll never forget our first Easter Sunday. The praise team kept stopping during the first two songs. I wondered why. Then I realized that the drummer, still wearing off his Good Friday and Saturday night binges, was playing completely different songs than the singers were singing.

More than just because they're funny stories, I share these because I see that early on in our ministry, enemy by enemy, we had to win on every level. Mountain by mountain we had to move every one of them.

In our early days, just forming a band seemed like a giant in the valley, and the big obstacle was finding one band member who could be sober. At the time, that was so monumental in my mind. I realize now that I had to overcome it or I wouldn't have gotten to the next place.

Giants come in stages and levels.

That's why God, who won't give us more than we can handle, doesn't give us the Goliaths in life before we fight the lions and bears on the back side of the hill—where we're still tending sheep.

Every conflict, if embraced properly, will reveal itself to you as a necessary step toward purpose and destiny.

PART 2

THE PLAN

God is an architect. He has plans. We are part of those plans.

This is why, as God planned the seven billion people alive on the earth today, He said, "Nope, no one can accomplish this purpose, so I have to create _____ (slip your name in here)." And the same is true for Mary. And John. And Juan. And Mariah. And Ron. How amazing is that!

What an awesome responsibility we each have to discover our individual purpose, because it will affect not only our lives but also the lives of other people now and for generations.

When we started our church, I believed God had given me three mandates that were a part of His plan for me as a pastor in Greenville. I'll discuss the other two later, but one of them was to break barriers of religious tradition that I felt were holding the body of Christ at large in a time warp. I just believed there were things that people held as sacred that really weren't that sacred, and that a lot of God's work had been stopped because people held on to things that were not as important to God as they were to people.

I admit it—I was a piece of work that basically defied everything that had ever been considered normal in the religious community of Greenville. I was intense. I was brash. I was fast paced. I was loud.

And I was a little bit crazy when it came to getting things done to complete the purposes and plans God had for our church. Like the incident with the air conditioners.

Greenville is very hot in the summer, and our little warehouse had no air conditioning. That may not seem like a big deal if you live anywhere in the world other than South Carolina, but when you're dumb enough to start a church in August in the dead heat of the South without AC, it's a deal breaker.

Fans can only do so much. I would preach with the sweat falling off me like rain. And even when I was shouting, the people were nodding off. That's why our first major fund drive focused on raising money to have air conditioners, because the building that we got such a great deal on (yeah, we eventually figured out why!) had neither heating nor cooling.

So a handful of bighearted people of very modest means set about to try to raise several thousand dollars to get portable AC units installed. In those days, with our income-challenged congregation, that might as well have been a million-dollar goal. It seemed insurmountable, but by God's grace and the amazing sacrifices of a few people, we did it.

The agreement with our landlord, which we had added on a page to the back of our lease, spelled out that once we brought these air units in, they would not be anchored to the ground but would be portable. This meant that if a day came when we got our own building, we could take them with us. In other words, they did not belong to the property owner; they belonged to us.

The property changed hands, and the new owner of this industrial park was an extremely shrewd businessman. Unknown to us, he tore the back page out of that lease and actually put his company imprint on the back of those air conditioners that we had purchased! This came at a time when we had finally purchased our first acre of land and were constructing our own small metal building.

When it came time to get our air conditioners, there was no proof that they had belonged to the ministry. Herein was my first legal dilemma, so I checked my Bible. I saw time after time that God used whatever the person had—Moses with his staff, Jesus with dirt and spit in Bartimaeus's eyes—to accomplish His will.

I couldn't afford an attorney, and so at that time, all I had was a lot of new converts, many of them with not much church background but with some valuable experience in, let's say, late-night acquisitions. The plan was in motion.

There's more to the story…but first I want to discuss several topics that relate to why enemies are necessary in the first place. What is going on in the world and in our personal lives is not random.

GOD'S BEAUTIFUL PICTURE OF YOU

I want to make sure we recall how important people are to God.

Our Daddy in heaven is really excited about the human race. And it's not only a group thing with Him, as in God "really loves humanity." No, it's very personal with Him. He's a Dad, you know. Here's how I like to think about this.

I suppose I'm like many dads in that in my office I keep some favorite pictures of my wife and kids. These are mainly candid shots of my family that make me laugh or even choke up. It's all very personal to me.

But, of course, just one picture cannot show everything about a person. It's only a representation of a moment in time.

I think God keeps pictures of His family in His "office" too, and I imagine that they may make Him laugh and cry. The difference is that God's pictures show the complete story of a person's life. Everything about the "photograph" is perfect, because that's the only way God can do things. And He doesn't need to Photoshop these pictures—they have no flaws.

To God, your life is a finished picture, beautifully painted on a canvas, and He is watching parts of it unfold every day.

The apostle Paul wrote, "He chose us in Him before the foundation of the world, that we should be holy and without blame before Him in love, having predestined us to adoption as sons by Jesus Christ to Himself, according to the good pleasure of His will" (Ephesians 1:4–5). In other words, God painted a picture of your life, looked it over, and just loved it.

YOUR ASSIGNMENT

Because you have a God-given purpose, this means the devil's painted a bull's-eye on your back. Satan does not like you, and his only interest in you is to figure out how to take you down. If you are headed toward completing the assignment God has given you on earth, Satan wants to stick out his foot and trip you up. You remind him too much of Jesus, and Satan wants nothing to do with Jesus.

As your assignment is revealed, the Enemy takes notice. When you begin to get a picture of what God wants you to be and do in life, that's when your enemy often shows up.

I've had many people over the years come to me or send me comments on my blogs about how they recently got saved, caught on fire for God, or maybe were believers for years but recently discovered their assignment in life. Many times they go on to explain how, almost immediately, it seemed as if all hell broke loose in their lives. My response usually goes like this: "Absolutely, because now you have purpose. As long as you were acting crazy in your sinning, Satan was fine with leaving you alone. But now that you've begun to bring order and boundaries to your life and you're heading in a positive direction, you're a threat."

Just as much as God intends for your assignment to be completed, there is an enemy who intends for it to never take place. That's why you can't ever give up. And that's why I'm doing my best to try to drive the "quit" straight out of you, because you can't be a quitter. There's too much at stake for the kingdom of God, your life, the lives of your children, and the generations to be born after you.

If you weren't on earth now for a God-established reason, the Enemy would take the bull's-eye off your back and stop target practice. What would be the point of harassing you?

It's good to have enemies and the trouble they bring—it means you're in the game.

YOUR PURPOSE IS TO *BE* SOMETHING

Your assignment or purpose in life is not just to *do* something, however. Your purpose is to *be* something.

When Paul wrote in his letter to the Ephesians that "we who first trusted in Christ should be to the praise of His glory" (1:12), he didn't tell them to just give God praise. He urged them to *be* a praise. This statement supports the principle that God seems to constantly put a priority on identity and not necessarily accomplishment. He created a picture of what you are called to be, so your life is to give glory to God.

Glory is not something that appears magically inside a building when you're having a good church service. In New Testament terminology, *glory* actually means "likeness" or "to resemble." In other words, for you to bring glory to God means that God is hard at work making you become something that resembles Him, something that more clearly bears His image. It comes as no surprise that this reality makes someone very upset.

The devil isn't concerned with fighting something that you're doing; he fights who you are becoming.

In the first thirty years of Jesus's life, while He was accomplishing many things as the son of a carpenter, we find no mention of any spiritual warfare coming against Him. But then John baptized Jesus, and the heavens opened to reveal His true identity. He was not really a simple laborer after all. He was not just Mary's son. He was the Son of God. And it wasn't until God's picture revealed Jesus's true identity that the Enemy immediately said, "I must challenge that." So, sure enough, after His baptism, Jesus was promptly led into the desert, where He was tempted by the devil for forty days.

Now, remember what the heavenly Father had said about Jesus when the Holy Spirit descended on Him at His baptism? "This is My beloved Son" (Matthew 3:17).

Read carefully what the Enemy said to Jesus to tempt Him:

"If You are the Son of God, command that these stones become bread." (4:3)

"If You are the Son of God, throw Yourself down." (4:6)

The devil said, "If You *are*…," not, "If you *do*…" The testing came at the point of Jesus's identity. The same is true for you.

> ### Real trouble will not come in life to challenge what you're doing; it will come to test who you are.

When the accusations started to fly against me after the collapse of our program to help single moms, I had to endure the trashing of my good name and character. I am Ron Carpenter Jr., which means I am carrying on an identity and reputation for the Carpenter name established by my father. Some of the qualities associated with that name included honesty and responsibility. It was not in my repertoire to be a liar and thief.

You can't imagine how I wanted to fight back in every way to defend my good name. But to get in the mud with every critic and fling it around would have made me look just like them. So I had to keep my manners and often shut my mouth.

Many people miss this point, because when challenges come, they get so focused on trying to save their reputations and making everything look right that they miss how the Enemy wants them to lose their identities in the process.

Can you fight through a battle and win? It depends on your definition of winning. God's definition of winning a battle has nothing to do with how much money you recover or the status you gain. God's definition of winning is fulfilled when you fight the battle and, after it's over, you are even more established in the identity He designed for you.

Whatever identity God has established for you, that's what you are, and battling an enemy will bring that identity to light when you face and defeat that enemy.

Your battle with the Enemy isn't over your stuff; his fight is to try to make you out to be something different from what you really are. If the Enemy can paint a different picture to the world than God did of who you are, he might succeed in stymieing the gifts God put in you or knocking you off course from fulfilling God's purpose for your life.

GOD DOESN'T WEAR
A WATCH!

In my personal crisis relating to the program for single moms, even though I was beginning to grasp why an enemy could benefit me, I still kept asking God, "But isn't there some better way? This pain that's draining all my resources—is this really necessary?"

I've learned that God does answer questions. But He does so in His way and according to His timing. I know—this causes huge frustration for us because, to us, time is a really big deal! I mean, we think time is about the most valuable thing imaginable. And the more timesaving devices we have and the faster everything moves, the more desperate we become about the value of our time.

You are probably muttering to yourself right now, "Come on, Ron, get to the point! I don't have all day to wait on you. Speed up!"

With most of what happens in life, we want to pull up in the drive-through lane, place an order, have it handed to us in a bag, and drive away—in sixty seconds or less.

We must understand that God isn't held by time. He's not captive to time and space; that's what makes Him God. But He absolutely cares about time, in fact, because you were brought into this world at a very intentional, specific, purpose-filled, deliberate natural time, with a supernatural purpose. He does operate within our lives within times and seasons, and a new season won't come until a previous season completes its purpose and you've accomplished all that God intended you to do in it.

The Bible says,

That which is has already been,
And what is to be has already been. (Ecclesiastes 3:15)

That's an amazing statement because it shows the difference between living in time and living outside of time. God does not live with us within time, so He is not growing old and changing with age. God is not frustrated with what we are frustrated with because our "clocks are ticking."

If we are to understand why an enemy might be necessary, we need to get a grip on something very important about God: He can take years of our precious time, maybe decades, to accomplish something in us that's important to Him.

All of this has to do with a critical principle of how God's kingdom works. The things of God have small beginnings, often so small that they go unnoticed.

THE DEED'S IN THE SEED

You and I are much like seeds.

Twenty years ago, two green Bible school students felt called to drop some Jesus seeds into Greenville, South Carolina. One of the mandates for ministry that Hope and I felt strongly about, as I've already mentioned, was to take on "religious tradition." The other two were to confront racism in the church and to seek to help break the bondage of poverty in this region. It took a long time for those seeds of our vision to become shoots that you could barely see above the ground. But now some of these seeds are good-sized bushes—and still growing.

Seeds contain promise, and ultimately they have to be challenged, pressed, and, yes, have dirt kicked on them to produce. They must have water and sunlight and be allowed time to bring forth the potential hidden inside them by their Creator.

When the Bible talks about the principle of a seed, we are aware of the laws of nature and how seeds are designed to function. Of course what Jesus said about this is particularly memorable:

Behold, a sower went out to sow. And it happened, as he sowed, that some seed fell by the wayside; and the birds of the air came and devoured it. Some fell on stony ground, where it did not have much earth; and immediately it sprang up because it had no depth of earth. But when the sun was up it was scorched, and because it had no root it withered away. And some seed fell among thorns; and the thorns grew up and choked it, and it yielded no crop. But other seed fell on good ground and yielded a crop that sprang up, increased and produced: some thirtyfold, some sixty, and some a hundred. (Mark 4:3–8)

The fact that an enemy has surfaced in your life is an indicator that there's unborn seed in you. The enemy doesn't show up because of what you're already doing; the enemy shows up to steal what is yet to be born. That's why the theme of this book is so vitally important for you to grasp: *the fact that an enemy has arisen in your life is an indicator that a seed is about to manifest itself.*

Jesus said, "Most assuredly, I say to you, unless a grain of wheat falls into the ground and dies, it remains alone; but if it dies, it produces much grain" (John 12:24).

Understand this: A seed can produce fruit only when it is resisted. It is the job of the soil to resist the seed to produce and bring out what's on the inside of it:

But we have this treasure in earthen vessels, that the excellence of the power may be of God and not of us. We are hard-pressed on every side, yet not crushed; we are perplexed, but not in despair; persecuted, but not forsaken; struck down, but not destroyed—always carrying about in the body the dying of the Lord Jesus, that the life of Jesus also may be manifested in our body. For we who live are always delivered to death for Jesus' sake, that the life of Jesus also may be manifested in our mortal flesh. So then death is working in us, but life in you. (2 Corinthians 4:7–12).

When an enemy rises, God is allowing the resistance, because He knows what's on the inside of you and needs it to come out.

A seed is not the end of the life of that seed; it is the beginning of what that seed will become. In fact,

Everything in life starts in seed form.

When you see the word *seed*, think about potential. Everything that has to do with something or someone's potential is wrapped up in seeds. The impact will not be made by what the seed is; it will be made manifest through what the seed has inside of it. Whenever God has declared something over your life, He puts the seed of those things He has declared on the inside of you. That's why Ecclesiastes 3:11 says that God has put eternity inside your heart.

That's what the Enemy is after—he wants what's inside of you. He is after the dream that has not been born, the vision that has not come to pass. He is after the you that you can be, the identity and the life you're not living out yet.

This is one reason why people get frustrated with the Bible and claim that it is confusing. The Bible will say a thing to us that contradicts our conditions. We have one set of conditions we see with our eyes that is temporary, but we think it's here to stay. God, however, says another thing. God calls you an overcomer. It doesn't mean you are presently overcoming. God calls you an overcomer because He created you and put potential inside you for the very conditions you're facing right now.

The head chef can tell you all the ingredients in a five-star meal because he created it before anyone else was around to see the final product. He knows all the ingredients. He mashed them together with the ultimate end in mind of pleasing himself and glorifying his craftsmanship through how the meal is received.

Likewise, God knows what's inside you. If God says you're blessed, you may not feel very blessed, but God called you that because He knows what is in there. When God says you are victorious, it's not because at that time you are experiencing victory; it's because He knows there's a champion inside you. God knows the potential of the seed He has put in you.

Your enemy knows the potential of that seed too, and so he comes to steal that seed in many forms.

YOU ALREADY ARE WHO
YOU WILL BECOME

Now get ready to drop your latte! What I'm going to say next may require reading several times, followed by some serious thought before you can get your head around it:

Every day on earth you are actually becoming what you already are!

Here's what I mean by this: You and I are in the process of becoming what God has already declared us to be. This is exactly what happened when God said that Jacob was Israel. Of course God had to wrestle with Jacob in order to get him to become the person Jacob was destined to be (Genesis 32:22–32). That can happen to us too.

It was the same for Simon Peter. Jesus declared that Simon was already Peter, but then we see the relationship they had and all the mistakes Peter made while becoming the person God ultimately wanted him to be (Matthew 16:16–19; 26:33–35, 69–75; John 18:10–11; Acts 10:9–16; Galatians 2:11–14).

God's intent was for Job to have a double portion of the life he had, and God used all the things the Enemy was able to do to him to accomplish it.

The same was true for what Jesus went through. That's why the Bible says that had the rulers of the time when Jesus was crucified known what was about to happen, they would never have crucified the Lord of glory (1 Corinthians 2:8). That was Jesus's intended end, and God used the enemies to accomplish Jesus's purpose on this earth.

These examples should give you comfort about how long it's taken you to discover this amazing principle. God has already declared certain things and events to be in your life, good or bad—even enemies—to take you to your intended end.

FROM THE END TO
THE BEGINNING

God knows the end from the beginning (Isaiah 46:10).

As I began my walk with God and I read that scripture, I thought it meant that God knew the difference between the two. I did not understand the powerful, life-changing impact this scripture (in addition to others like it) would have on my thinking, my decisions, and the paradigms and root systems I would challenge in my life. This scripture means that God knows the end of a thing when He begins a thing. This is awesome: He knows the destiny of a person when He breathes life into that person.

God is not waiting to figure out what the outcome will be when He begins a creation process. Did you catch that? He starts something having already designed and destined the outcome.

So the fact that He started the area of your life where you're now facing a challenge from an enemy is the very evidence that He'll bring you through the battle to complete the thing. That's why Paul made the statement, "He who has begun a good work in you will complete it until the day of Jesus Christ" (Philippians 1:6).

How could Paul make such a strong, bold, confident declaration about God finishing everything in my life? He could because Paul understood that anything God has started, He's already finished, because He works backward from the end, not forward from the beginning. Remember, He predestined you. He went to your end first, and He designed your end before He started your beginning. That's amazing!

If He has already started something in your life, it has to be brought to completion; otherwise God would never have started it. If God has started repairing relationships, God has completed repairing those relationships. If God has started bringing you out of debt, God has seen you debt-free. If God has started breaking addictions and bad habits in your life, God has seen it brought to completion.

If God has started something in your life, He already knows that it has been completed. And He wants you to begin seeing it the same way. As the Bible says, through faith and patience we inherit God's promises (Hebrews 6:12).

God said it. You can believe it.

THE REASON FOR TESTING

Many people think that when they are going through a test in life, God is trying to teach them something. I disagree, because a good teacher does not use a test to teach you something…

A test measures what you already know.

So why would we think the greatest teachers of all—Jesus and the Holy Spirit—would operate any differently?

After final exams in college, my friends and I would always celebrate because we knew this signaled the end of one semester and the beginning of another, as we moved closer to becoming college graduates. The exams challenged us to prove what we'd learned. They stood in the way of our new identities—ultimately "college graduates." This is why I say so emphatically that if an enemy enters your life, go ahead and throw a party, because the enemy is signaling a transition. It's your indicator, a blinking sign, that the next season in your life is about to roll around.

I once heard author Mike Murdock say that your friends encourage you, your family humbles you, but only an enemy can promote you.

So in the time of testing, God is evaluating what you have learned during the previous season of your life. And you have to overcome or pass that test, which often comes in the form of an enemy, in order for God to advance you to the next level of your purpose.

Many people get so frustrated during a time of testing because they feel as if the heavens are brass, God won't respond, and God isn't answering their prayers. When you're in your greatest time of testing and the pressure's on, it seems like heaven's the most silent.

Remember, in grade school as in life, the teacher is always silent during the test. Not only will the teacher not respond and speak to you, he'll typically not allow others to speak to you either. I had to recognize during my own battles that the silence and isolation were by design, so I was forced by the Teacher to focus on the test.

A test forces us to focus squarely on what we know to be true. The enemies you're facing right now may be there because God recognizes you've lost focus and it's stopping you from accomplishing your purpose. The problem, as well as the test, forces you once again to refocus on what God is trying to do in, with, and through your life.

WHAT IF I REALLY
HAVE MESSED UP?

Can rebellion and foolishness—a series of really bad choices—wreck the destiny God planned for you?

Many minds far greater than the one I haul inside my skull have tried to explain how God's many qualities, such as omniscience and omnipotence, integrate with the free will of people. How does all of that work?

I'm not going to try to fool you—there's a deep mystery to this. But I will unashamedly point out some key scriptures that shed a lot of light on this topic.

Paul wrote to the Ephesians, "In Him also we have obtained an inheritance, being predestined according to the purpose of Him *who works all things according to the counsel of His will*" (1:11, emphasis added). And, of course, Paul also wrote the famous words, "We know that all things work together for good to those who love God, to those who are the called according to His purpose" (Romans 8:28).

Those statements indicate to me that God is bent on making sure His intended end for us is accomplished. But maybe the most telling scripture is this:

You can make many plans, but the LORD's purpose will prevail.
(Proverbs 19:21, NLT)

These Bible passages, and others I could list, convince me that God's intended end will be reached in spite of your decisions. God, in His greatness, has a way to take your right, your wrong, your good, your bad, your apathy, your ambition, your mistakes, and your successes—to take it all and make it fit the picture of your life that He crafted from the very beginning.

Having said that, however, I do think that...

God is not a God of the lottery; He's a God of levels.

In life, you don't get from God what you think you deserve; you get what God thinks you can manage. A new enemy will arise as a key indicator that a new level is about to dawn on your life.

This principle was illustrated in the parable Jesus told of the servants who each received ten minas from their master (Luke 19:11–27). The master commended the servants who showed responsibility with their actions.

Some people are just waiting on God to drop manna out of heaven right into their laps. Best I can tell, they're not doing much of anything to work out their salvation with fear and trembling (Philippians 2:12). Instead of working, they're waiting for their big ships to come in, but so far they haven't even touched the oars in their little boats. I'm not smart enough to even guess how God can work with that scenario—but I'm sure somehow He does!

What I do know is that God is a God of levels. He moves us from one level to another—from faith to faith, from glory to glory (2 Corinthians 3:18).

In my calling as a pastor, I've had to demonstrate my faithfulness in leading ten people before I could lead one hundred, or five hundred before one thousand. In our first church, I had to keep the shower curtains clean and the metal building swept out...before we could have the brick buildings with real walls. Everything was a test of my faithfulness on a prior level, before God moved me to a higher level.

As I've already said, at the conclusion of one level, there's a test God gives to see what we've learned before we are promoted to the next level. And if the test doesn't go so well, He will find a way to let us take it again.

He's good about that. I know from experience.

GOD IS A CLOSER

God isn't a bad start-up venture. He does not start something and then try to figure it out along the way with no plan, no resources, no relationships for success. In fact in Jeremiah 29:11–14, He said the very opposite:

"I know the plans I have for you," says the LORD. "They are plans for good and not for disaster, to give you a future and a hope. In those days when you pray, I will listen. If you look for me wholeheartedly, you will find me. I will be found by you," says the LORD. "I will end your captivity and restore your fortunes. I will gather you out of the nations where I sent you and will bring you home again to your own land." (NLT)

Our part in this is to cooperate with "the plan." Jesus had something to say about completing what we start:

For which of you, intending to build a tower, does not sit down first and count the cost, whether he has enough to finish it—lest, after he has laid the foundation, and is not able to finish, all who see it begin to mock him, saying, "This man began to build and was not able to finish"? (Luke 14:28–30)

This scripture really helps us understand God's intention; He's all about finishing.

When a baseball team is ahead by a run or two in the final innings of a game, a pitcher will be brought in to preserve the victory. This guy is a closer, often a big, mean-looking fellow with a three-day beard who throws hard strikes and looks like he wants to bean every batter! God is not mean, but He is the ultimate "closer." He has the "stuff" to make sure you win.

"YOU CAN KEEP THE AIR CONDITIONERS"

I promised to finish the story of the raid to claim *our* air conditioners.

At this point I was just a young pastor in my early twenties who had a genuine desire to live an honorable life worthy of my calling, but I also had learned that when you're in this line of work, you have to go the extra mile to earn people's trust and the right to lead them.

So, here I was, already facing my first lawsuit. I've already shared with you about greater lawsuit giants and enemies that came later, but this was my first level of enemy. The air-conditioner lawsuit wasn't my Goliath, although it seemed so at the time. It was more like I was a David preparing to meet his Goliath someday by taking aim with his sling at trees on the backside of the mountains of Galilee or maybe even taking out an occasional lion or bear to protect *that* flock.

I recruited a few of my, well, "least saved" members and had them meet me at two o'clock in the morning, like a special ops team wearing camouflage in the middle of the night. We were brilliant. We lay down in the back of a truck, wore eye black, and used hand signals in place of verbal communication. We were God's soldiers, part of the kingdom military preparing for battle.

The team traveled that night through darkness and through forgotten back roads, led by their reverent pastor with his hat turned around backward (the official redneck battle cry, where I come from). Then we unbolted and hauled our air conditioners back to their rightful home, on God's property, at God's new church!

It was midmorning the next day when, as a humble man of the cloth, I walked up to my new church home, only to be greeted by local police officers who, in their defense, were simply doing their job. They confirmed who I was and escorted me, in front of some of my "elders" (most of them with two first names), to their squad car.

As they were reading me my rights, all I knew to do was scream, "They're miiine! They're miiine!"

Somehow we were able to talk the policemen, who wanted to cuff me, into understanding that this was not a criminal issue but a civil issue and that I didn't need to be locked up for it. They agreed with me, leaving it up to the courts to decide.

The landlord filed a lawsuit to get "his property"—the air conditioners—returned.

Our day in court came, and I had to represent myself because all our money had gone to pay for the air conditioners! The landlord had a collection of highly paid attorneys and paralegals who carefully built his case. At the time, he seemed like the biggest enemy I had ever faced: no air conditioners, no air conditioning. And in August in South Carolina, if you don't have air conditioning, you can kiss your church good-bye, no matter how great a preacher you are.

I had very poor paperwork (at best), and the landlord came in looking like he was bringing a case to the US Supreme Court. Right at the end of his attorney's barrage of well-articulated closing statements, the judge slammed the gavel, declared it a frivolous lawsuit, and dismissed the case and me! I wasn't sure exactly what had happened, but I did know it meant we got our air conditioners back.

As I was leaving, the judge turned and looked at the landlord and said, "Uh, not you, sir. Sit down. I have a few things to say to you."

I found out afterward that the judge lit into him for a solid thirty minutes, spanking him for trying to steal air conditioners from a church.

This victory was my bread. Little did I know at such a young age the Goliath battles I would later face, but I had now seen God give me victory and that was "fuel" for my future battles.

Even then, in the beginning days of our ministry, I began to learn the principle that adversity, seen with the right perspective, can be a strengthening tool to propel us toward our destinies.

Or at least bring some cool air to a room so that people can hear the Word of God!

PART 3

THE TARGET

et's review a few key ideas:

- God is a planner.
- Your purpose on earth is a part of God's planning.
- God has an enemy who is also your enemy.
- The Enemy wants to keep you from completing your purpose and comes against you.
- God promises victory over the Enemy and also promises progress toward accomplishing the next season of your purpose.
- But the Enemy has no morals or ethics and only wants to destroy you. You are his target.

I thought I had endured some fairly significant adversity until I entered a *real battle.*

In 2004, as soon as word got out about the scam regarding the single moms' program, my trial in the court of public opinion began. As so many people find out these days, once you come under suspicion, regardless of the validity of the charges, you might as well go climb on a cross because the crucifixion is under way.

I was put on trial in newspapers and radio talk shows. Every time I stepped out the door at home or the office, a reporter with a camera crew was there.

Even after nearly fifteen years invested in helping people and trying to be a blessing to our community, almost overnight our motives were questioned on all sides.

We became a target. The battle was on. But I didn't really get it yet.

When a class-action lawsuit was filed against me, people began to take sides. There was great suspicion on the church campus. I felt like I was a prisoner in the ministry I had founded. When I walked by an office, I didn't know what the people working there had heard, what they believed, whose side they were on. So what had always been a pleasant journey of "hellos" in the office hallways now became a journey of anxiety and suspicion.

There was no pleasure in work, in the pulpit, and at home. This enemy I was facing had attacked me on all fronts, and I had no safe place. There was no rest or peace.

Longtime friends didn't call as they used to.

Our kids, harassed by taunts, rolling eyes, and passed notes, had to change schools several times.

I could not go grocery shopping, eat at a restaurant, or pump gas without fielding stares, angry accusations, and hand gestures.

I wasn't fully aware of it, but my back had a huge bull's-eye painted on it. The enemy arrows were flying.

I also didn't fully understand it, but even though I was struggling big time, in God's reality, I was well on my way to a season of significant blessing. That didn't keep me from bleeding, however.

Here is something you need to know, and it may sound odd:

You are not really blessed when you get a new fishing rod or dress. You are really blessed when people are talking about you like a dog!

I'd better explain that one.

ARE YOU SURE YOU WANT TO BE BLESSED?

How do you and I know when we're blessed? Most people think they're blessed when they start accumulating things—stuff like large tires with shiny rims or a big-screen TV or the dream house on the cul-de-sac. Or maybe it seems like a blessing if the media start saying nice things about you or your accomplishments, and you end up in a "Who's Who" book somewhere.

Even in church we think a blessing is like that. I've heard that perspective in all kinds of churches: black or white, Pentecostal or Baptist, small or large—you name it. Someone asks, "How ya doing?" And the answer is, "Well, I'm blessed and highly favored." What people mean is there's a state of goodness in their lives.

Too bad that's really not the truth! Sadly, few Christians have ever truly known what being blessed entails.

You need look no further than Jesus to find the definition of blessed. Wouldn't you say that among you, me, your pastor, your family, and Jesus—He's probably the most credible source? Here was His succinct summary: "Blessed are those who are persecuted."

Say what? Would you mind repeating that, Jesus?

Imagine if we didn't know this was Jesus speaking, and it was just some regular person we hang out with every day. Be honest—wouldn't you and I think, *Man, this guy's not very spiritual. He needs help*? Why would we think that? It's not in our nature to embrace persecution from enemies, because we have an earthly perspective, not God's perspective.

We are more interested in that scripture that talks about the blessing being so big that we can't contain it. That's the scripture we all want on our refrigerator doors or on our bathroom mirrors. So what's with this verse, the one that says we're blessed when we're persecuted? Who could build an ad campaign with a slogan like that? Believing this particular scripture means we have to shift out of the paradigm of equating being blessed with something like getting a certain kind of car.

Let's take a closer look: "Blessed are those who are persecuted for righteousness' sake, for theirs is the kingdom of heaven" (Matthew 5:10).

When you decide to pursue what God wants for your life, a persecution will come against you. This doesn't mean, necessarily, that you will be boiled in oil! Persecution often sounds something like this:

- "Well, who do you think you are?"
- "Nobody in our family is going to..."
- "You need to quit acting like you're not one of us."
- "Why are you trying to be better than everybody else?"
- "Oh, excuse me, you got saved, so now you're too good to do what we've always done when we hang out?"

Embracing the meaning of this scripture and how it plays out in everyday life is an enormous paradigm shift for most Christians. In Possum Kingdom English, this truth sounds like this: "Blessed are you when they talk about you and cut you off and roll their eyes and pass notes. God said you're not blessed when you get a big-screen TV. You're blessed when people revile you; when they hate your guts; when you're persecuted."

I've learned something that doesn't sound very good but is often true:

If you ever discover what people hate about you, you'll discover what's valuable about you.

Years ago I was at a meeting in another city, and I had to stay over Saturday night due to some travel challenges. I couldn't possibly get home in time to preach in our church on Sunday. It was a rare opportunity to attend a church in that city. I had no idea where to go, but I got in a cab that morning and told the driver to take me to the most talked about church with the most hated preacher in the entire city. I wanted to go to the church everybody in the Christian community was envious of and could not stop gossiping about. The taxi driver looked at me with a strange, confused look—but he knew exactly where I needed to be dropped off!

Did I do this because I like controversy? No. In fact, I love peace. But I knew this principle: The church that the driver took me to that day would be the one in the city that's doing something. The pastor who can't find other pastor friends in his city is a likable guy, but because he's so intent on pleasing God first and God only, people leave other churches and go to his because they know their lives will see breakthroughs.

This principle will change your life if you get hold of it. In church, though, we've got it backward. When an *enemy* rises up against us and we have people treating us like dirt, don't we come into our small groups and ask for prayers, or ask to meet with the pastor and the elders, or find people to commiserate with us and tell the devil to leave us alone and go away?

Imagine if the shepherd boy David, after hearing about Goliath, had gone to the temple, started a prayer chain, rode his donkey down to the local coffee shop, and talked with his accountability partners about big, bad, mean Goliath and how they all should pray and be in agreement that Goliath would simply go away. David's future and the future of generations to come probably would have been aborted simply by his inability to see Goliath from God's perspective.

Your perspective on persecution will impact your process, plans, and potential.

To understand this concept of what it means to be truly blessed, you've got to understand the nature of persecution and get God's perspective on it. I've been pastoring and traveling all over the world, speaking in both churches and corporate environments, and I've noticed some things that are very common among people, no matter what the environment or culture.

In general, the common hate the uncommon. The impure hate the pure.

The unrighteous hate the righteous. The lazy despise the diligent. People want what you have, but they don't want to do what you did to get it. They simply are more comfortable hating you because you have what you have; it's a safer alternative to challenging themselves to rise above their mediocrity.

When you've got people misunderstanding you, lying to you, and coming against you, God says He wants you to start praising, because the fact that they're talking about you means *you are blessed*!

THE DEVIL HATES
YOUR POTENTIAL

Anyone operating in God's purpose, anyone with a future, anyone who takes territory must understand that warfare is involved.

Once God declares that movement is about to happen in your life, enemies creating winds and waves will show up to rock your boat. Jesus's disciples found this out in a memorable way:

> Now it happened, on a certain day, that He got into a boat with His disciples. And He said to them, "Let us cross over to the other side of the lake." And they launched out. But as they sailed He fell asleep. And a windstorm came down on the lake, and they were filling with water, and were in jeopardy. And they came to Him and awoke Him, saying, "Master, Master, we are perishing!"
>
> Then He arose and rebuked the wind and the raging of the water. And they ceased, and there was a calm. But He said to them, "Where is your faith?"
>
> And they were afraid, and marveled, saying to one another, "Who can this be? For He commands even the winds and water, and they obey Him!" (Luke 8:22–25)

Opposition is a given for anyone who follows Jesus. The day when Jesus calmed the storm on the Lake of Galilee, everything was pretty calm in the lives of the disciples until Jesus declared they were all going "to the other side."

When I speak of the necessity of an enemy, I'm referring to the presence of an enemy at all times letting me know there is unrealized potential inside me. You do not see my whole life manifested in me yet. Our enemy doesn't know all the details either, but he knows who's behind the plan—so the Enemy seeks to take us down as quickly as possible.

In the parable of the seed, notice that, when the seed is sown, Satan comes "immediately" (Mark 4:15). The Enemy knows that seed sown means a huge harvest of good things, for the kingdom of God is just one growing season away. So he takes action quickly.

When we talk about seed in the biblical sense, we are talking about the Word of God. The Word of God always brings a picture of the future that is greater than what is around you. You may be in the midst of turmoil, but God will give you a word of peace. You may be broke and unemployed, but God will give you a word that you are blessed.

These are examples of what I call a *faith image.* It is an image God gives you that you can fulfill by your faith. You can bring it to pass and make it a living reality.

With this in mind, notice how Jesus went on in the parable of the seed to more clearly reveal the Enemy's tactics against targets like you and me:

> The sower sows the word. And these are the ones by the wayside where the word is sown. When they hear, Satan comes immediately and takes away the word that was sown in their hearts. These likewise are the ones sown on stony ground who, when they hear the word, immediately receive it with gladness; and they have no root in themselves, and so endure only for a time. Afterward, when tribulation or persecution arises for the word's sake, immediately they stumble. Now these are the ones sown among thorns; they are the ones who hear the word, and the cares of this world, the deceitfulness of riches, and the desires for other things entering in choke the word, and it becomes unfruitful. But these are the ones sown on good ground, those who hear the word, accept it, and bear fruit: some thirtyfold, some sixty, and some a hundred. (Mark 4:14–20)

Anything in seed form is in its easiest state to destroy. It's a whole lot easier to pull up an acorn that is just starting to sprout than to uproot a forty-year-old oak tree.

Even now you may be thinking about your life and wondering, *Why in the world am I having such conflict in my life?* It's not your present conditions that are the focus of the battle. The battle is over your position and identity in God's eyes, the purpose you're called to fulfill.

Most of the time, your enemy knows and recognizes your potential better than you do.

SEEING IS NOT BELIEVING

Jesus, master teacher that He was, used a memorable miracle to teach His disciples a lesson on faith.

Later on in the day when Jesus taught about the seed and sower, He and the whole crew got in a boat on the lake. He told His disciples to sail to the other side. Then He fell asleep. You know the story—a great storm came up, and the disciples freaked out. Finally they woke Jesus up, saying, "Teacher, do You not care that we are perishing?"

I love His reply. Jesus stood up and spoke to the winds and waves and said, "Peace, be still!"

Then He turned to his disciples and asked them, "Why are you so fearful? How is it that you have no faith?" (Mark 4:38–40). In other words, He was saying, "I just got through telling you how this works. I told you the Word of God is supposed to get in a man's heart, but Satan comes immediately."

The Enemy does this all the time. He creates a scenario that casts doubt on God's Word. Jesus's point was that He had told them they would make it to the other side. In essence, what He was saying to the frightened disciples was, "I didn't tell you how we would get there. The waves might rip the boat apart, and we may have to swim! No, I didn't give you every detail of how your future would unfold, but I did tell you that we would get to the other side!"

What mattered was His word. They had gotten themselves in trouble by looking at the wind and the waves, instead of remembering the promise.

Most people get caught in the middle of the same predicament the disciples found themselves in. We've been promised the "other side," but we lose faith when it becomes clear that we can't hold God to the details of how He will get

us there. We can't forget that there is an enemy that, somewhere along the journey, does not want you to make it to God's intended end.

Remember, this enemy is necessary to remind you that there is something
worth fighting for. Don't let go of what you heard, no matter what your enemy
created for you to see. That's why the Bible makes it clear that "we walk by faith,
not by sight" (2 Corinthians 5:7).

God knew you'd have battles, and that's why He comforted you by remind-
ing you of the outcome of your battles: "He who is in you is greater than he who
is in the world" (1 John 4:4). Keep in mind that it's your enemy's assignment to
set up conditions around you that contradict what's in you, to reshape life's conditions so that they contradict the promise God made concerning your life.

That's why the Bible says, "Faith comes by hearing, and hearing by the word
of God" (Romans 10:17). Faith comes by *hearing*, not by *seeing*. Most people
think the opposite of faith is doubt. Not true.

The opposite of faith is sight.

We don't live by what we see, but the Enemy wants you to live by something
that you saw, something that contradicted what God said about you, because
even he knows that what's in you is always greater than what's around you.

Don't take your battles too personally. It's not about you; it's about what is
in you.

DREAM KILLERS

Do you remember the story in the Old Testament of when the spies came back from checking out the Promised Land—two spies with a good report, but ten with a bad one (Numbers 13–14)? The ten tried to weaken Israel's passion for the Promised Land. We all know about Joshua and Caleb because they were the two. Do you know who the ten were that had a negative report? No, because nobody cares.

There's an enormous pool of negative enemies who will come across your path in life. Negative people never stand out significantly when history is recorded; they just blend in. Negative people, allowed to speak into your life, will become agents of destruction of your purpose.

An enemy will always try to weaken your passion for your dream.

One day Jesus was passing through a town, and the blind man Bartimaeus was standing on the side of the road, with a dream to have his sight restored (Mark 10:46–52). He started screaming to Jesus, but the disciples told him to be quiet. When the disciples tried to weaken his passion, what did Bartimaeus do? He knew he had to get out of the crowd and be different from everybody else. This was his moment; he didn't know if he'd ever get this kind of chance again.

Bartimaeus called out, "Jesus, Son of David, have mercy on me!"

The disciples shot back, "*Shh,* be quiet."

"Son of David, have mercy on me!"

Sometimes you've got to get more radical when the negativity and criticism start to surround you. Don't let them shut you up! You need to birth that dream in you.

When the prophet Habakkuk said to "wait for" a vision that's coming (Habakkuk 2:3), he didn't mean you should sit in your recliner and stare at your watch. That word *wait* in the Hebrew means "ambush." So the Bible says that while you're waiting on your vision, be as you would when you are planning to ambush something: you're already prepared for it when the opportunity comes. You don't wait until an enemy gets right in front of you and then scream, "Where's my gun? Where's my gun?" No, you're waiting to aggressively attack when your moment arrives.

If you are passively living life, it's going to pass you right by and your enemies will tear you to pieces.

When you wait for a vision, you don't know when *yet* is. You don't know when *yet* is because Jesus is the "Lord of the harvest" (Luke 10:2). You're the lord of your seed, but Jesus is the Lord of your harvest. Therefore you don't know when He is going to call it in.

That's why Bartimaeus went crazy. This was his once-in-a-lifetime moment to change his life, and he knew he wanted to attack as though he'd waited his whole life, so he started screaming.

He was waiting to ambush his miracle.

DEFRIENDED BY THE DEVIL

f your enemy knew that all he was doing was making you greater by bringing adversities into your life, he would back off and delete your name from his e-mail list. He would no longer want to be your friend on Facebook either. He would just forget you altogether. Why? Because all he is doing is bringing about God's intentions and being used as a pawn of God, a catapult to propel you toward your destiny.

The Bible declares that all who are born again are adopted sons of God (Ephesians 1:5). In other words, it was actually Jesus's crucifixion that multiplied Him from one to many. His greatest battle and enemy brought about His greatest fruitfulness and multiplied His influence.

> If by the one man's offense death reigned through the one, much more
> those who receive abundance of grace and of the gift of righteousness will
> reign in life through the One, Jesus Christ.... Therefore, as through one
> man's offense judgment came to all men, resulting in condemnation,
> even so through one Man's righteous act the free gift came to all men,
> resulting in justification of life. (Romans 5:17–18)

By this "one thing" that came on Jesus, everyone—you, me, all of us—was declared innocent. There was a multiplication of Jesus's power and influence and everything that He was, which arose out of the Enemy's greatest attempt of all time to stop Him.

That's what gave me strength in realizing that in my darkest day and through my greatest battle and biggest enemies, *everything* that was great in Ron was about to rise up through the trial I went through.

How about you? I submit that the same thing can—and will—happen in your greatest battle.

———

We are targets of the Enemy, and he's painted a big bull's-eye on each of our backs.

More important, there's someone else in the picture who always has our backs covered. As Paul wrote:

Who shall separate us from the love of Christ? Shall tribulation, or
distress, or persecution, or famine, or nakedness, or peril, or sword? As it
is written:

"For Your sake we are killed all day long;
We are accounted as sheep for the slaughter."

Yet in all these things we are more than conquerors through Him
who loved us. (Romans 8:35–37)

More than conquerors! I like the sound of that.

PART 4

THE ENEMY WITHIN

There's a big difference, as I've shared, in being delivered from something and being truly freed from it. When these wounds surface (and eventually they always do), they can be crippling.

Not every enemy you face will fire arrows at you from behind a bush or plant IEDs in your driveway. Sometimes the toughest foe to conquer is the one living beneath your own skin.

It's true. Sometimes we are our own worst enemy. Or maybe more accurately, something inside us we can't seem to conquer, some flaw in our character or an addiction we can't whip—that's what rises up to threaten our destiny. So that means, no matter the cost, we have to take it down.

When I faced the challenge with the single moms' program, it seemed I had enough external enemies to keep me engaged until Jesus comes again. But the enemy that came closest to taking me out was my own dearly held ways of doing life.

I may not have been a workaholic, but I had some poor boundaries around my passion for ministry. My intense, driven lifestyle had worked for me for many years, but I know now that eventually it would have ruined my health and cut my ministry short.

Enemies within us can be wounds or patterns that were rooted in our childhood or that were created out of a difficult relationship. Or sometimes such an enemy is a bent toward a certain perversion or a propensity to be drawn into a destructive lifestyle.

An internal enemy is potentially more dangerous than an external enemy because the bruises to your soul are hidden. You may have survived incest, rape, or divorce. Those are horrible experiences, but they are in the open. An internal enemy may go undetected, silently doing damage for decades before suddenly making an angry appearance in a relationship.

We all deal with learning how to overcome things that happened in an earlier season of life. Most of us have had things happen to us, usually early in life, that sowed negative seeds in us that sprout root systems that eventually can sabotage our future. So something that happened to us at ten years of age grows and ends up leading to not-so-pretty consequences when we're thirty-five years old.

I've always been somewhat athletic and had health on my side, but as the pressure and stress over the crisis of the single moms' program built during a two-year period, I began having excruciating headaches. They were take-any-kind-of-pill-you-can-think-of-to-calm-the-pain-type headaches. I was waking up with headaches, going to bed with headaches, and staying up all night with headaches. I ate aspirin like candy.

One night it felt as if my skull was about to crack, so Hope drove me to the emergency room. The hospital staff ran tests and found that my blood pressure was through the roof. An elderly ER doctor told me, "You could die walking from your bed to the exit doorway of this room."

High blood pressure is called the silent killer because many people don't know they have it. That wasn't true for me: I was having unbelievable head pain. And even though I wasn't overweight and worked out three or four times a week, I had the blood pressure level of someone living a life of gross self-neglect.

During that same time period, I also developed a hiatal hernia behind my chest cavity that was inoperable, but I had to be hospitalized so they could look at it through a scope. This hernia was also exacerbated by stress, and I had to take many types of medication for this condition too. The headaches and hernia made my quality of life miserable. I had something inside me that wanted to destroy me. The doctors told me that if I didn't make immediate lifestyle changes, I was not looking at a happy ending.

The problem was that I didn't know how to change. This enemy inside me, this unhealthy pattern of dealing with life I'd perfected over many years, caused so many problems that I was forced to break and change lifestyle habits that eventually would have taken me to an early grave. This internal enemy of my health made me stop and evaluate my eating habits, my ways of mishandling stress, and my inability to get adequate rest. It began to change what I would say yes and no to. It built a whole new level of boundaries in my life because my health—and ultimately my purpose—was at stake.

The beautiful answer to our problem with internal enemies is what Jesus accomplished at the cross. The prophet Isaiah said it best. This is my paraphrase: "He was wounded for our transgressions [outward cuts and bleeding on the cross for outwardly obvious sins], He was bruised for our iniquities [our internal sins and flaws that we hide from others]" (53:5).

And it's not just our healing that matters. Whatever God does in you, it's in part so that you can turn around and do something similar for someone else. The Enemy knows that if you ever uproot and defeat that enemy within, you'll be free to help others win the same battle. Paul wrote to the believers in Thessalonica: "You became followers of us and of the Lord, having received the word in much affliction, with joy of the Holy Spirit, so that you became examples to all in Macedonia and Achaia who believe" (1 Thessalonians 1:6–7).

Praise God that today my headaches are gone and the symptoms of the hernia have almost totally subsided. So here again it's that same wonderful truth—our afflictions can work for us, just as Paul promised, to bring an "exceeding and eternal weight of glory" (2 Corinthians 4:17).

ROOT PROBLEMS

If you're wondering how an internal struggle in your life got there, there's a good chance you can trace it back to a hidden enemy from years ago. And know this: if you do not confront it, it has the ability to derail you and eventually destroy you.

Years ago my wife and I brought home a Labrador retriever when he was just a puppy. He was ambitious and aggressive, so we had to train him to keep from running away when we let him outside. At the recommendation of a dog trainer, we installed an underground electric fence and put a special collar on the dog. When he approached the electric fence boundary, the collar would beep. If he moved closer to the border, then he would receive an electric shock. The electric charge wouldn't hurt him, but he certainly didn't like it.

It took only a few shocking experiences before he had been conditioned to stay behind the fence. He had learned where that boundary was, and as he grew up, he wouldn't go anywhere near it. In fact, over time, he even grew scared of sounds similar to that beep, because the sound of this enemy was embedded in his memory.

One day I wanted him to hop in the back of my truck and come with me to the gas station to pick up some things. I took off his collar and started leading him toward my truck. And that's when something happened that revolutionized my understanding of internal enemies. As I approached the boundary, the dog stopped. He sat down and whimpered. When I tried to get him moving, even though I had taken his collar off, he wouldn't move past the boundary. The memory of his battles with his enemy and the pain of those events held him captive. I literally had to pick him up and harness him in order to get him across that line.

Even though geographically, physically, and in reality the dog was free from the boundary, mentally he was still locked to it. He was so yoked, so trained in his mind by painful experiences, that he couldn't go beyond a certain line.

Are you allowing an old enemy of internal struggle to hold you behind its lines for the rest of your life? If this is the case for you, the great news is this: you have a God who can free the collar from your neck if you'll call on Him to defeat this enemy.

I'm not urging you to ignore a weakness that may have been passed down through generations and now rests inside your flesh. I'm not urging you to live a religious life publicly and a tormented life privately. I'm not urging you to experience great displays of power in church, only to go home and be once again overcome with weakness. I am urging you to have a committed heart: commit yourself to a walk with God where even your flesh bows its knee to the will of what God wants in your life.

People may hold things against you, but God will forgive and forget it all. He'll open up a brand-new life and show you wonderful things that you never knew were in you and that nobody has ever recognized.

Maybe God is speaking to you right now. Maybe tears are even flowing down your face as you fight this battle alone because you have a problem that you don't want anybody to know about. Maybe you're the kind of person who holds the family together or leads the company; you have created an image and everybody looks up to you. But inside there is something eating away at you that no one else knows about.

I want to assure you—God is not angry at you. The human race is fallen, broken, and full of problems, and if you are alive, then you have your share in this. The Bible says,

Many are the afflictions of the righteous,
But the LORD delivers him out of them all. (Psalm 34:19)

There you have it. Even the "good, nice, holy" righteous people have struggles! But our hope for healing and strength is in the Lord, who is our Deliverer. Don't delay—go to God for help with your inside enemies.

THE DEVIL MADE
YOU DO IT?

I need to make clear that when I talk about an enemy within that needs to be defeated, I do not mean your garden-variety personality quirks and bad habits. To overcome such things, mostly what you need is discipline, not a battle strategy. I have observed this countless times:

**A lot of people get more spiritual when they
should get more disciplined.**

I have known some people who go to their ATM machines and start rebuking the devil when there are not sufficient funds. This situation has more to do with too many trips to Pizza Hut and the nail salon than with the Enemy! It's not the devil that needs rebuking—it's undisciplined use of the credit card.

Some Christians like to blame their bad habits and daily frustrations on the devil: "I just don't know why I did that. I guess the devil made me do it."

My response to that? "Give the devil a break! No, you thought about it, you meditated on it, you planned it, and then you did it."

Frankly, sometimes it's easier to superspiritualize something and blame the devil than to understand a need or personal flaw and take ownership for it.

There are some areas of your life where you just need to make some changes in the way you do things and then develop the discipline to follow through.

The battle within is typically more serious and has greater ramifications related to your life purpose than the fact that you twirl your hair when you're nervous or slurp your soup.

FIGHTING THE FLESH

Can what the Bible defines as our "flesh" (wanting to live life our way instead of God's way) become a serious enemy?

Yes, but we certainly don't have to be dominated by fleshly desires! We all have decisions to make about what will dominate our thinking and determine our belief systems.

Your flesh has desires all day long. If you focus on those desires, your thoughts will bring you into captivity to what your flesh wants. But you can reverse-engineer this principle: God has desires too. If you focus on *those* desires, then your spirit will bring you into captivity to the will of God. Your spirit and your flesh both exist, so your mind (your soul) gets to choose which one to listen to every day.

Someone might say: "I told God I wasn't going to sleep around anymore, but I did. I don't know why I did it!"

I would shoot back, "Well, when you're over at her apartment at 4:00 a.m. sipping wine, burning candles, and listening to let's-get-it-on background music, it doesn't do much good to rebuke the devil. You should have thought about different plans for the evening in advance of your date!"

The apostle Paul wrote, "Make no provision for the flesh" (Romans 13:14). Some people could be delivered by tomorrow if they would quit giving their flesh so many opportunities.

You love God, you're saved, and you want to live right, but you say, "That thing keeps grabbing me." It wins because your flesh had a desire and you meditated on it long enough to allow it to become a consuming thought; then you put yourself in a position to sin.

This is one principle of discipline I often teach men (I'm told it works for women too):

Put lines of separation between your weaknesses and yourself.

This really is another way of saying, if you stay away from the fire, you won't get burned.

When I was growing up, my best friend's father bought and sold pornography. As a young teenager, I'd go to this friend's house, where there must have been over ten thousand porn videos in the basement.

I watched those for years, so you can imagine the struggles my wife and I had coming into our marriage. She had been raped as a teenager, and I was a testosterone-filled freight train. We collided.

Thankfully, after many years of God's grace in our relationship and some great marriage counseling, we're strong as a couple. But since I had this propensity to indulge my flesh in a certain way, for the first several years of my ministry, when I traveled, I would call ahead and ask the hotel staff to remove the television set from my room. This was a line between my weakness and myself.

This practice drew critical comments from a few pastors I knew. "Don't you believe God has delivered you from porn?" they would say.

My answer was simple: "I'm not sure, so I'm not going to take the chance and allow it to take down what I've built up."

I made it impossible to get to porn, because I knew that if I did that long enough, there would come a day when it would lose its hold on me. That fleshly desire would be starved and dead if I would not give it a chance to feed on anything.

Your flesh still has desires it wants to fulfill and things it wants to do, and it doesn't have your best interests in mind. Your flesh lives only for the moment, and if you put it in a position to sin, it will seize every opportunity to do so.

That's why, if you're struggling with a particular sin, you've got to separate yourself from it and make it impossible for your flesh to get it.

LIVE FOR THE LONG TERM

Does the God who *is love* hate anything?

Yes. One thing God despises is when someone throws away a long-term blessing to satisfy a temporary desire.

In Malachi we read, "Jacob I have loved; but Esau I have hated" (1:2–3). Those are strong words coming from God! Here's what happened: Esau had the birthright in his family, but because he was hungry, he traded that inheritance for a meal—a bowl of beans. Esau gave up the rewards of his future in order to satisfy his empty stomach.

That's pretty much how it still goes with people—it's the way of the flesh. The flesh is all about gratification—not tomorrow or next year but *now*.

The apostle Paul implored us to "walk circumspectly, not as fools but as wise, redeeming the time, because the days are evil" (Ephesians 5:15–16). The root word for *circumspect* is *circle*. Life involves cycles, and we should live each day knowing that decisions made now will come back around and revisit us.

A foundational principle of the Christian life is sowing and reaping, so a spiritual person always lives with the harvest, or the future, in mind:

Today's decisions are tomorrow's reality.

I strongly urge you not to do something that God hates! Don't let short-term passions destroy long-term blessings. Don't give up your steak dinner for a bowl of beans.

WINNING THE BATTLE WITHIN

Now, ultimately, do you root out a hidden enemy lingering from your past? Where do you find the power?

There's an obscure verse in the Bible that offers surprising insight on this question. This is what Isaiah 10:27 says:

It shall come to pass in that day
That his burden will be taken away from your shoulder,
And his yoke from your neck,
And the yoke will be destroyed because of the anointing oil.

There it is. If you're battling an internal enemy, your peace can come from finally realizing the power of this summary statement:

The anointing destroys the yoke.

An ox is a large and amazingly strong animal. During Bible times, oxen were used for breaking up hard ground with plows so crops could be planted. The farmers had to do this to prepare the soil so the seed would grow.

No one could teach a full-grown ox to take a harness. By that age, its strength would be too great for anyone to tame it. That's why an ox had to be yoked at an early age. A farmer would put a yoke around a young ox's neck. As the ox grew up and experienced life, all the ox knew was the weight of that yoke. So, over time, the yoke was just a part of the ox's pattern of coping with life. The ox had the physical strength to break out of the farmer's control, but the animal didn't know this and became obedient behind a plow.

Yet the Bible says that even such an oppressive, confining yoke could be destroyed by "anointing." What does that mean?

Some people think anointing is some sort of spiritual lightning bolt that comes without warning out of the heavens, but that's not the meaning of this verse. The Hebrew word for "anointing" in Isaiah 10:27 can actually be translated as "fatness." The idea is that as the ox grows bigger and stronger, its very size—"fatness"—eventually cracks and destroys the yoke.

What this means for you is that God will not break your yoke (destroy the power of your hidden enemy) from the outside. He will break it from the inside. Certainly God *can* miraculously remove something from your life, but most of the time, you'll find that freedom will come through your consistent, daily growth—in your increasing "fatness." God will make you so *big,* spiritually speaking, that whatever bondage may have held you in your youth will break and will no longer hold you in adulthood.

This is true, of course, if you seek this anointing.

This enemy, this struggle in you, the one that's plagued you most of your life, is hidden, but you also have a hidden strength. Are you accessing your hidden strength—growing it, nurturing it, feeding it, exercising it to allow it to become so fat on the inside of you that it eventually has to break the yoke on you?

Many people believe that if God is going to free you from something undesirable in your life, there's going to be a moment of power in a praise song, a good church service, or prayers of an intercessor to free you forever. Here's the truth, however, that you won't hear in most churches: that's not how God works.

The enemies within are usually not destroyed in a moment in a church prayer line. You may get temporary relief that way, but enemies are usually destroyed over a period of time.

That's how you battle and ultimately defeat an enemy within.

WHEN YOU ARE WEAK...

Everybody has a dominant gift, but did you know that each person has a dominant weakness? And did you know there's a bull's-eye painted on it? Throughout your Christian life, you'll find that you're usually not going to be attacked in the area of your strength. But your weakness has a target painted on it, and you've got to understand your weakness so you can guard against attack.

I like to describe the challenge this way:

**An enemy is anyone or anything that
feeds your dominant weakness.**

King David had a dominant weakness—it was women. Here was a man after God's own heart. He loved God. He led others in praising God. But he had something dangerous inside him that just didn't want to die, and it manifested itself in a relationship with a lady named Bathsheba.

David struggled the majority of his life to get a grip on that weakness, and that weakness was passed down through his bloodline. His son Solomon had seven hundred wives and three hundred concubines (1 Kings 11:3), and that was his downfall.

The apostle Peter's dominant weakness was that he was subject to other people's opinions. Whatever group Peter was in, he became one of them. When he was with the disciples, he'd say things like, "Lord, I am ready to go with You, both to prison and to death" (Luke 22:33). Peter wanted Jesus and the other disciples to have a good opinion of him.

Many years later the apostle Paul had to confront Peter about his bent toward being a people pleaser. Peter was eating with Gentiles, but when his Jewish friends showed up, he then distanced himself from the Gentiles in order to be with Jews (Galatians 2:11–14).

People who go from group to group and relationship to relationship, seeking the approval, affection, and admiration of that group, have no foundational core. This was Peter's dominant weakness.

What is your dominant weakness? Maybe you're undisciplined. If you need to become a better steward of your money, the Enemy will bring people into your life who are foolish spenders, which will encourage your weakness.

When you include someone in your life who is trying to strengthen that thing God is trying to remove, you've got to view the person as an enemy of your future and your purpose.

If you're a man with a weakness in the area of sexual irresponsibility, you'll attract or seek out a certain kind of woman who will feed it.

If your dominant weakness is substance abuse, you will gravitate to certain numbers on your cell phone when you're depressed, celebrating, or experiencing any emotional high or low. In fact, let's be honest: you probably have that person on speed dial. Simply put, your dominant weakness does not want you to kill it.

Your dominant weakness wants you to pursue the people and situations that feed it, and simultaneously it will pull you away from the people who won't justify, validate, or tolerate it. This is a pattern you can trace all the way back to the first man, Adam. When Adam sinned, after sewing himself a pair of fig-leaf pants, he fled the presence of God (Genesis 3:8). He wanted to get away from the One he knew would not justify, validate, or tolerate what he'd done. That should explain why we are the way we are, since Adam is a part of our distant family tree!

You've probably had, or currently have, a person in your life who wants desperately to help you destroy your weakness, and that's the person you'll find yourself shying away from when you see him or her. While you will avoid that person whenever possible, your weakness-fed desire will draw you to the person who will help to create the ideal conditions and environment for it to grow and manifest itself.

Don't fool yourself into thinking you don't have a dominant weakness, because you've got something that if left alone will sabotage your future.

WEAKNESS IS NOT
NECESSARILY SIN

Let me clarify something important that many people get confused about when it comes to weaknesses: not all weaknesses are necessarily sinful.

For example, if you have had a lot of dreams but no discipline, and people have heard you talk about your dreams for twenty years but have never seen you do anything about them, that's a weakness but not necessarily a sin.

The problem is, while it goes largely unnoticed (and apathy is not a very noticeable sin), it's a dominant weakness that will be a handicap in realizing your purpose.

There are some people who don't know when to quit talking. There are other people who don't have any self-control. Those are more obvious things people might call flaws. However, what do you do if, ironically, strength in one area is also a weakness in other areas?

I'm in that category, and I've found that many leaders are in the same predicament. I have an innate capacity to get focused on a goal and grab hold of it like a saber-toothed tiger. When I do that, it's almost impossible for me to be shaken off, come hell or high water.

The irony is that this steely determination is also my weakness. I can get so focused on where I'm going that I don't see what's right in front of me.

In one situation a few years ago, thankfully, I was able to escape the weakness. I came in one day to have our regular weekly staff meeting. Now, usually in these meetings we talk about the future, about goals, about change; we share vision and strategize about how to get there; and we make and refine plans. On that particular day, however, I sensed the Lord directing me not to do that. "Love on them," I heard the Lord whisper.

So all I did in that meeting was listen and speak to the needs of others in the room. People started to cry. God started moving. It was a wonderful thing.

God was saying to me that day, essentially, "Son, quit looking so far out in the future that you don't see that you've got people right next to you who need your prayers and your love."

Being a visionary and a trailblazer are strengths, but they can also be my blind spot.

What is the double-edged sword for you? Maybe you're incredibly effective at being persuasive, and this makes you successful as a salesperson. But perhaps the mouth that lets you close the deal is the same one you don't know how to shut up, and so you are perceived as controlling or gossipy. If that's the case, your strength is also your weakness.

A weakness is not necessarily a sin. The sin comes in allowing the weakness to produce bad fruit in your life.

DEPRESSION IS NOT
THE ENEMY

I do not view depression as a weakness per se, and it's certainly not an enemy as I am defining one in this book. But because of the almost epidemic presence of depression among people today, I want to include some discussion of it.

The word *depression* has always seemed to be off-limits when talking about Christians. The church has incubated a culture where Christians aren't supposed to be depressed. So we have churches in all parts of the world where many people are depressed but hiding it, taught to put on their church faces and tell everyone how blessed and highly favored they are.

Depression is in the soul part of us—not the spirit or body (although there can be physical ramifications). That sounds simple enough, but most people don't understand that happiness and sadness don't come from other people or from acquiring more stuff; these are discovered in your mind.

Here's something I want you to think about:

**If you can beat it in your mind,
you can beat it in your life.**

I know rich people who want to shoot themselves. In fact, I can take you to palaces and pulpits and everything in between where the people should be ecstatic, but in reality they are in tears and wanting to end their lives.

I'm not coming at this topic as a clinician or as a psychologist. I believe, however, that my more than two decades of pastoring and all the experience that I've had counseling people in difficult times give me insight into the subject.

As Christians, so many of us were taught that the day we got saved, everything became okay and all our old problems, habits, and ungodly lifestyles vanished instantly. Because of that, it's as if we ignore the reality of what we're going through, thinking things will magically get better, and in many cases, it seems as if people check out of their minds instead of renewing their minds.

When it comes to depression, I do believe there are chemical deficiencies in people that require a physician's help and perhaps medication. But sadly, in so many cases, suffering individuals won't seek medical assistance because they feel something's wrong with them spiritually if they do, as if they aren't demonstrating enough faith to overcome the problem.

This is bad thinking. We have no problem with sending people to the doctor if their livers aren't functioning correctly, or if they have hypertension, or if their bodies don't regulate blood sugar properly. But somehow, if they have trouble in their minds and they go to a doctor, they're viewed as spiritually *less than us* and needing more of God.

Ridiculous! It's time to hit this issue head-on.

Life takes us through seasons (Ecclesiastes 3), but we seem to get seasons and weather mixed up all the time. When we get a little rain, we assume it's a stormy season, and when we get a ray of sunshine, we think it's a season to rejoice. Let me clear this up, simply and succinctly.

In general, summer will be a great vacation season, a time when school is out and people are more relaxed. For families, there will be vacations, great times at the beach, cookouts, and other activities. It's a season of fun and relaxation for most kids. However, I promise it'll rain a few nights. Just because the season is a great season doesn't mean it's immune to a bit of bad weather.

So when you're evaluating the season you're in, recognize what's typical of the season and what's simply a bit of inclement weather for a short period during the season. If you know not to be tempted to fall into a full-blown depression when a storm hits for a couple of days during a time when you're supposed to be feeling like a champion, this will help you not short-circuit God's plan for the season you're in. Here's a way to look at this:

Learning how not to get too high on life's highs or too low on life's lows will help keep you stable.

I've had seasons that have been filled with failure, and I cried a tear or two. Sometimes I've cried way more than that, just as I've celebrated significantly when I've had seasons of accomplishment. It's called life, and I have learned to manage the ups and downs because the truth is that life brings all of it.

Feeling down or depressed is a part of being human. I know from experience.

WHEN LIFE KICKS YOU IN THE GUT

Back in the spring of 2010, I got to the lowest point I had been in for a long time. This should not have been the case, but our emotional states don't always match the outward facts of our lives.

Our church had tackled the largest deficit we'd ever had, and we were experiencing one of the greatest recoveries as we came out of it. We had a new satellite campus starting, a charter school for at-risk kids, and many other amazing things breaking out.

However, the trauma and pressure of the years before those victories had taken their toll. I got to a point where I sat on a stool on a Sunday morning and spoke to my congregation like never before. I was burned out, and through my tears I asked them to allow me to struggle and break down and work through my depression in front of them, rather than leaving for a while.

They were amazing, as always, and gave me great support. It was the scariest time of my years in ministry, because until then I'd never had feelings that I couldn't control. They were overwhelming. I actually wanted to quit, to somehow get out of the pressure I was in.

One night before this, I had come to a place that scared me. I was in an overwhelming "I don't give a rip" place, all alone because Hope and the kids were out of town. That feeling alarmed me, so I immediately put praise and worship music on for about five hours while I lay on the floor, refusing to get up until the feeling left me. The emotion made me want to close the blinds, think about all the trouble and failures I'd ever had, and stay locked in the feeling. So I had to change the atmosphere until the feeling broke.

All that happened on a Saturday night, five hours before I had to get up and preach on a Sunday to a worldwide congregation and inspire them to fulfill their potential!

Not a good place to be.

It doesn't matter what degrees you've earned, where you came from, or who your daddy is—no one is exempt from having a down day. You are not the exception, and I can tell you that with passion, because I thought I was.

I had thought wrongly that I could go through trouble unaffected. In fact, I really thought it was a gift, that I was anointed to endure things that would crush other people. I'd praise God for it, but I was deceived into thinking I was going through the turmoil of my life and nothing was penetrating me.

My point: When we need help, we need to seek it. There's no shame in that.

We don't need to cover up sadness. But we also don't need to let some blueness indefinitely discolor our visions for the lives God offers us.

GET RID OF THAT BOAT!

I love the apostle Peter because he showed us so much of his flawed human side. Impulsive, overly talkative, proud, two-faced—the list goes on. Of course, it brings great comfort to know that a guy with this kind of makeup could become a pillar of faith. There's hope for all of us!

Peter does provide a great example of something we all need to do from time to time: get rid of that boat!

I know I'll have to explain that.

Remember how Peter started off as a fisherman in a boat before he met Jesus (Matthew 4:18)? That boat represents, for many of us, a comfortable way of doing things, an old habit, an addiction, a crutch, a "sure thing," or a safety net if all else fails. We step out on faith, but we keep the boat around just in case. We have a plan B, and the entire time God is asking us to get rid of our plan B and make Him our only plan.

I think that, in Peter's case, the boat never really left his heart during the three or so years he spent with Jesus.

He walked with the Lord every day and shared meals with Him. He heard all of Jesus's teaching and saw all His miracles. And for a while his past was behind him.

All of a sudden, however, after Jesus went to the cross, Peter's past began to revisit him and the old lifestyle beckoned him. He went back to fishing temporarily (John 21:3). He went back to the boat.

Do you have an old lifestyle tempting you? Are you under pressure to do something that might look good today but that you know will be bad for you?

Think about Peter: What was it, through three years with Jesus calling him to a new life, that caused him to keep his boat around?

If we're being honest, most of us have been like Peter at some point when God called us to do something great and walk in faith with Him.

Don't rely on an old way of life to go back to if God has breathed a dream into your heart and a vision for an uncommon future into your mind.

Get rid of the boat!

Finances are one area where this principle shows up. If you're struggling financially and you get prayed for in church, I absolutely believe that within days God may use someone to send money your way for temporary relief. But poverty has nothing to do with income; it has everything to do with thinking. Poverty isn't a financial state of affairs; it's a state of mind.

If you give a cash windfall to someone who's been poor throughout life, the money will quickly vanish. Why? Because life is lived on levels. If you leap over several levels of financial responsibility and strength, you don't learn how to be wise with your money. That's why so many lottery winners are broke again within eighteen months. They can't maintain the level they were thrust into because of their inadequate knowledge and practice.

——

When I think of how an internal enemy can take us out, King David comes to mind.

This guy seemed the picture of strength. He had encountered every imaginable enemy, starting with the one named Goliath. Later he had to fend off the maniac Saul, and then he faced one battle after another throughout his life as he fought to establish and maintain his kingdom.

And on top of it, David was a worshiper, a man who stayed close to his Master.

As long as David was fighting battles outside himself, he fared well. But then he decided to take some R and R from the battlefield, during the season when "kings go to war." Lallygagging around his palace, he caught sight of the naked Bathsheba, and an internal enemy, rooted apparently in his own laziness and lust, led him into adultery and, ultimately, murder and shame.

An enemy within brought the great King David down.

That doesn't need to happen to you. Remember, you're much more powerful than you think. You may have some enemies lurking inside you, but there's someone else at work in your interior world—the Holy Spirit. And "He who is in you is greater than he who is in the world" (1 John 4:4).

PART 5

WEAPONS OF MASS DESTRUCTION

Some enemies you just do not see coming.

One afternoon, when I was feeling incredible heat on all sides from the single moms' program situation, I drove out of Greenville into the countryside. Eventually I came to a four-way stop. I was surrounded on all sides by open space—not a sign of anything man-made in any direction. There was no traffic, so I pulled to the edge of the road.

My style of doing ministry and living life had been to push hard and, when necessary (which was most of the time), take the role of leader. I was really a guy who had no other voices speaking into my life. I had no real mentors because the higher you go in any organization, the more difficult it is to find somebody without an agenda to give you guidance. Also, as a leader, I thought I could not show any flaw or chink in my armor.

The only people, outside of my wife, who were even somewhat close to me all looked to me for leadership and encouragement. You can guess where that left me, now that I was the one needing some support: very *alone*. In this case the enemy that approached and threatened me was my own isolation, which as you will soon discover, is one of the Enemy's favorite weapons he uses to destroy us.

There I sat in my car, in the middle of nowhere, alone, wishing I had just one person I could call who could hear my hurt and disillusionment and offer some comfort. I scanned through the address book in my phone, seeing hundreds of "contacts," but there wasn't one person I knew I could call and just let all the pain hang out without possible repercussions on me and my ministry. The realization of my loneliness brought tears, and I cried hard.

I could have camped there on my self-pity and pain (and believe me, I did consider just starting the car and driving as far as I could go), but instead I turned to the Lord for solace. I was in a place where I knew that my only hope for survival was to once again desperately pursue a relationship with God.

I turned around and drove home.

I had slowly lost some of my fervor in the many years of giving my all in ministry. And since deep trouble had never hit my life until now, I had developed some bad habits of self-sufficiency. I desperately needed God, not just so I could have a pleasant relationship with Him, but so I could stay in "the game." I dove into Scripture, no longer just to find material for a sermon, but to find interaction with the living God. I began once again to carefully guard my personal devotional time, spending hours, instead of minutes, with the Lord.

I did all those things. And I also read some books and listened to people in my life whom I respected. One of them was my friend Mike Murdock, who said, "Every enemy in the Bible was beneficial." I thought about this over and over so many times. Something had unlocked. I was fascinated by the possibility that an enemy could result in so much good, but I had to test this idea in my own study of the Bible. And that's what I did—for months.

I also decided to get serious about finding some true friends and mentors. I began looking for men I respected who would not need to be impressed with or intimidated by me, men who would never have to depend on me for anything. That would allow them the freedom to not only care about me but also to tell me the truth.

This is how I was able to hold my own against this particular weapon of the Enemy, as well as the others I will discuss now.

I think that these weapons of mass destruction the Enemy uses to sabotage our purpose are ones that you, too, will have to take on at some point in your life. They're so dangerous because they usually don't show up as Goliaths.

Instead, at least in the beginning, they tend to be unobtrusive. They are often stealthy, silent, and disguised. Their appearance is gradual, and instead of mounting a frontal attack, they tend to snipe at you from behind over time and wear you down.

Your ability to distance yourself from some of these weapons, change others, and even kill a few off will determine not only how efficiently you fulfill your God-given calling and purpose on earth but also how much you enjoy the journey.

WEAPON 1: ISOLATION

Balancing being responsible and being relational is very difficult.

In Revelation, Jesus spoke to a group of Christians, and while He acknowledged and celebrated all the things they were doing well, He also chastened them, pointing out in one case that they had departed from their first love (2:4). Jesus was putting the priority on being relational over being responsible, implying that no matter how much you've accomplished, if the passion to accomplish doesn't come out of the priority for cultivating relationship, what value will your success have? He was helping us understand that everything we do should flow out of relationships.

Jesus said, "If you love Me, keep My commandments" (John 14:15; see also verses 21 and 23). In other words, "You'll have no problem if you've kept your relationship with Me up-to-date and current." Decisions made in isolation tend to erect silos in your life, and it's a dangerous pattern to begin, because over time you choke out voices that are assigned to speak into your life.

> **Isolation is potentially lethal because
> it leaves you to deal with your internal
> struggles by yourself.**

This issue of the danger of isolation shows up in Scripture. Do you recall how the prophet Elijah took on the prophets of Baal in a "my God is bigger than your god" competition? Elijah ended up calling fire down from heaven and eventually wiping up the floor with those other prophets. But then Queen Jezebel, who was greatly displeased with him, said to Elijah, "Let the gods do to me, and more also, if I do not make your life as the life of one of them by tomorrow about this time" (1 Kings 19:2).

After hearing this, Elijah ran away and went under a tree, crying to God, "It is enough! Now, LORD, take my life, for I am no better than my fathers!" (1 Kings 19:4). He took himself to a remote place and lost all perspective. That's what can happen when you isolate yourself.

Eventually God rescued Elijah and informed him that he was not alone in Israel. There were many others ready and willing to lock arms with the prophet.

The point: don't let the Enemy get you alone.

WEAPON 2: THE IMMATURE KID IN YOU

Psychologists have told us for years that every child has emotional needs, and when these needs aren't met, there is potential for issues to surface in adulthood, particularly in relationships.

I am certainly not a therapist, but I have been deeply entrenched in the people business for more than twenty years of ministry. And I have concluded that if needs are not met in childhood, seeds are planted in the soul that may take ten, twenty, even thirty years to germinate and bear fruit.

A seed can fall from a tree and start to grow in the wrong place in the yard. If it's not removed, in time it can produce a tree and a root system that spreads under concrete and tears up even the foundation of the house.

If we have never dealt with our unmet emotional needs, they have the potential to produce root systems and bear behavioral fruit that can undermine relationships and wreak all kinds of havoc. If as a child you felt unloved, then as an adult, you will quite likely believe the lie that you are unlovable. And anytime we base our actions on falsehoods, we sabotage our futures.

We cannot ignore pains and difficulties of youth as if they never happened.

If these things have locked you into a place of emotional immaturity, your future depends on letting God deal with these places within you so that you can reach your potential.

Another way to say this is that inside every King David, there is a little kid David—some issues, maybe from early in life, that have not been attended to. And that little kid, if he's not managed, groomed, mentored, ministered to, and cared for, will want to sabotage the king's role in life. The kid will want to rise up and cause the king to make little-boy decisions in a season that demands adult decisions.

Be on guard. Our enemy loves to take the early wounds of our lives, throw in lies about them, and then coax us to act foolishly out of hurt and unresolved anger.

We are called to grow up, so "that we will be mature in the Lord, measuring up to the full and complete standard of Christ" (Ephesians 4:13, NLT).

WEAPON 3: OUT-OF-CONTROL FEELINGS

God gave you your feelings as a gift. How wonderful it is to feel happy! How wonderful it is to feel affection! How wonderful to feel the touch of a child! How wonderful to look a loved one in the eyes! How wonderful are the feelings of a Christmas morning!

But there is a downside to feelings: Let's say you have a bad day or get some bad news, and then the predictable sad or angry emotions come over you. When that happens, you need to take some time and separate yourself from any decision-making process until you've had time to regain control over your feelings. Never let emotion have dominion over a decision-making process; let your decision-making process have dominion over your emotions.

**Don't let the Enemy manipulate
your emotions to get you off track
and off purpose.**

The problem is, too many of us make long-term decisions based on the feelings we have about short-term problems. We find ourselves battling a problem, and all of a sudden we start thinking, *I'm tired of this* or *I've had enough,* and then we make a rash decision that has long-term effects.

It's critical to rein in feelings that are out of control. And never has there been a more compelling example of the danger of living out of feelings than the story of Jacob and Esau.

When we read about the forefathers of our faith, the names of Abraham, Isaac, and Jacob come up. No one talks much about Esau. The irony is that Esau actually was the firstborn and had the birthright. We should be hearing about Abraham, Isaac, and *Esau*. As we've already seen, Esau acted on short-term feelings, and he was hungry, so he traded his inheritance for some fast food.

So many people, in a short-term need to satisfy a desire to feel better, sell their futures in moments of passion, hunger, or lack. They may crave attention, so they have affairs that ruin their marriages. They've run out of money before they run out of month, so they abuse their credit cards. The list goes on and on—short-term pleasure obtained in exchange for long-term purpose and satisfaction.

When people do that, their feelings become the enemy of their destinies. Through Moses, the Lord said: "See, I have set before you today life and good, death and evil.... Therefore choose life, that both you and your descendants may live" (Deuteronomy 30:15, 19).

The fact is, life is decision driven. God has a plan prepared for us, but we have to make choices, and we must manage our emotions or they will become Goliath enemies in our lives.

Paul exhorted us that there is no law against self-control (Galatians 5:23)!

I can't tell you how many times during the several-year ordeal concerning the single moms' program my emotions were screaming, *Forget it! You don't need to put up with this!* Only the grace of God kept my attention riveted to my life purpose: *I am a pastor, which means I minister to people in the name of Jesus.*

Many Sundays I put a smile on my face and stood up on our church platform and talked about the goodness of God and urged people to let Jesus change their lives, all the while knowing that my name in the community was mud and that people I had given my life to were saying hideous things about me. I would finish the service and walk out the back door of the sanctuary. As soon as it closed behind me, the tears would run down my face. I was overcome with emotion because I knew that once again I had made it—I had preached the gospel in spite of the pressure I felt. And I would have to go by myself to a quiet place and deal with the pain and questions. I could not have done that on my own. I received supernatural help from God.

So I believe that a real mark of maturity is when you don't respond to feelings in an overly emotional, knee-jerk way. We need to keep the long-range focus in mind and make decisions that will lead to that intended end.

WEAPON 4: FALSE IDEAS ABOUT YOURSELF

A wrong perception of yourself is a weapon the Enemy will use against you. False ideas about who you really are in Christ are like land mines *you* plant in your life that *you* step on at the most inopportune times.

An interesting example of this is the life of Mephibosheth, whose story also reminds us that just because you're in an environment of greatness doesn't mean you feel great about yourself.

Mephibosheth was the crippled son of King David's friend Jonathan. When David came to power, he had Mephibosheth brought to the palace, but Mephibosheth apparently had a poor image of himself and felt unqualified and unworthy. He said, "What is your servant, that you should look upon such a dead dog as I?" (2 Samuel 9:8). Whoa! Did Mephibosheth need therapy? His perception of himself almost disqualified him from the table of royalty that was his due, because he was a descendant of royalty.

This is an important distinction for your life. You see, most of the time internal struggles about your identity are in your mind. You can be in a really good place but still feel lame. You can be invited by the CEO to join her table but feel unworthy of sitting there.

Perhaps everyone else sees you as successful, but you see yourself as a failure. Everyone sees the good you do, but you know the wrong you've done—so you wallow in shame. You know where you've failed and what you're guilty of and what you think you're incapable of accomplishing. So your attitude about yourself stinks.

The fact is, it is impossible to be great at everything—in spite of how cool and together others may appear. I believe that if Mephibosheth had taken a peek underneath the tablecloth, he would have discovered that all the other guests also had "lame feet" in some form or another—flaws or deformities inside them. They simply had their "lame feet" hidden by the tablecloth because they had arrived at the table before Mephibosheth.

We all know people who are good at one thing and bad at another thing. I've seen people prove to be good at managing money but poor at raising children. Others know the Bible front to back but cannot offer the barest encouragement to someone who's struggling. You'll always have areas in life where you feel lame, especially compared to others, but you can't let the poor areas go unconfronted.

What Mephibosheth had to realize was that he had the right to be at that table even with lame feet. And much like him, every one of us has been through events that left us feeling lame. But God invites us to sit at His table, lame feet and all.

After growing up in Possum Kingdom, I can assure you I have had many Mephibosheth-type experiences.

I remember one time in the early days of our church when we began growing from a small group of broke, busted, and disgusted people to a congregation that included some middle- and higher-class people. One day a prominent businessman who had become a member invited Hope and me to dinner at his exclusive country club.

I had heard of the club but never imagined I would go there. And when I showed up, my wardrobe didn't fit their expectations—I was stopped at the door because I wasn't wearing a jacket.

I ran back to the car for a coat. This was just the beginning of my Mephibosheth experience.

There followed numerous awkward, uncomfortable introductions and a long walk to our table past staring guests.

When it was time to eat, we encountered an elaborate seven-course plan. I'll never forget what happened next: I left Hope at the table chatting and went to the buffet line to get some soup. When I dipped the serving spoon into the bowl, it came up with the biggest shrimp I had ever seen. I had no idea God made shrimp that big—I thought that's why they called them shrimp!

Like a kid let loose after hours in a candy store, I ran back to the table and said to Hope, "Baby, check this out! They put food in the soup!"

I was dumbfounded. *Food in the soup—what will they think of next?* Lemme tell you: in the Possum Kingdom corner deli, they don't serve shrimp in soup!

Have you had an experience or two like that? Probably not! But all of us know what it means to feel inadequate as Mephibosheth did.

I encourage you to let the Word of God fill in your résumé. Don't let the Enemy feed you a bunch of lies about how "lame" you supposedly are.

WEAPON 5: HIDDEN FEARS

Too often the idea of having to battle an enemy builds up in our minds to be such a daunting task that we refuse to face it. We delay the battle. We run and hide. Our "self-talk" becomes increasingly fear based.

Fear probably stops more people from accomplishing things for God than any other factor. Jesus often urged His followers to "fear not." Paul wrote that we are to be "anxious for nothing" (Philippians 4:6).

Yet people worry about the smallest things and let fear of "what might happen" cripple them into a passive ineffectiveness.

Most of what we worry about will never happen. We get all worked up over unsubstantiated information and other lies whispered into our minds. Our chief enemy is known as the "Father of Lies," and his reputation as a liar is well deserved! He loves to see us cowering because of the awful things that might happen to us.

This creates a distinct disadvantage because, while the Enemy is waiting patiently and conserving strength for the battle, we are becoming emotionally drained and weakened by fear. We are not able to draw on strength and resources from others, because our fear is hidden.

Shedding light on hidden fears will eradicate them. Fear is a dark thing in life, so what better way to destroy darkness than to flip the switch on the light found in God's Word? When we understand God's view of any situation, that truth will confront our fears. We see what we really are facing and can respond with wisdom and courage.

WEAPON 6: RESURRECTION OF AN OLD THING

Ever find yourself in a spot where you have an old problem that you thought was dead, but it apparently was only asleep and is now revisiting you?

This is not unique to you. Imagine how the children of Israel felt when they were standing at the shoreline of the Red Sea and needing God to part the waters. Pharaoh had decided to pursue them, and all of a sudden the Egypt they left was at their backs. They heard the footsteps pursuing them from a life they had thought was over, the sound of an enemy they had thought was already dead to them (Exodus 14).

Have you ever been terrified because something that you thought had left your life for six months, six years, or sixty years is suddenly back? Maybe your enemy is an old wound you thought had healed. Maybe it's the vicious words from an old relationship.

If God has destroyed your enemy in a past season, He doesn't want you resurrecting that enemy in your present season. But He certainly can help you destroy it in this season if it tries to revisit you. The Egypt that went down the first time went down a second time. The Bible says that those who will call on the name of the Lord will be saved (Joel 2:32), and that principle works anytime, especially when an old enemy tries to reengage you in battle.

**The resurrection of an old thing
is common at a point of breakthrough
and transition.**

That's when an old enemy will surface to try to pull you back. But God is not surprised—He's in the business of rescuing people over and over again before they leave this earth.

Do you have an old lifestyle tempting you? Are you under pressure to do something that might look good today but that you know will be bad for you? Don't rely on an old way of life to go back to if God has breathed a dream and a vision in you for an uncommon future.

WEAPON 7: IGNORANCE

Everyone wonders how much power the Enemy has, and many times as believers, we give him credit for things he simply doesn't have the power to do in our lives. However, there is one area where I believe Scripture supports the idea of the Enemy having permission to wreak havoc in your life.

I know theologians love to debate this subject, and I realize I won't convince them of my interpretation with a couple of paragraphs, but that's not my intent. My goal is to help you identify, overcome, and defeat enemies in your life. So the first step to defeating and conquering a problem is moving from ignorance to knowledge, because knowledge is power.

Without getting into a doctrinal debate, I'll say this: I don't believe the Enemy has power in any area of the life of a believer unless he has earned and gained influence in it. In those areas, I believe he does have permission to traffic.

Stay with me, because this is a critical point in our discussion.

Where do I believe Satan traffics? The Bible says he has been reserved in darkness:

> The angels who did not keep their proper domain, but left their own abode, He has reserved in everlasting chains under darkness for the judgment of the great day. (Jude 1:6)

Now, many times in the Bible, *darkness* is the word given to describe ignorance. Additionally, a reserve is a specific area that has been marked off. Where there's no knowledge of the truth, therefore, that area is marked off for the Enemy. This is where "people are destroyed for lack of knowledge" (Hosea 4:6).

The Bible also is clear that, as a man "thinks in his heart, so is he" (Proverbs 23:7). If your mind goes there, your life will follow. The fact is, to gain entry into my life and influence it, the Enemy will attempt to fire thoughts into my mind about an area where truth isn't prominent to get me to agree with his ideas.

Remember this: *if you believe a lie, you will live a lie.*

Over the years I have made some major bonehead choices. So I know the reality of this:

You can make a decision in one day that will take you five years to straighten out.

The truth is, you don't have five years to waste! God prefers to see you take five years building your future instead of correcting a mess. Pain is usually not God's first choice.

When I use the word "ignorance," I don't mean not listening to your teacher in class so you end up "ignorant"—not knowing the material. That's not a good thing, but the seriousness of being a bad student is nothing compared to being ignorant in the spiritual realm.

After we are born again and receive forgiveness and cleansing from sin because of what Jesus did on the cross, the lifelong process of "renewing the mind" begins. This is where the battle with Satan rages. Even though our spirits come alive and are new through salvation, our minds have to be renewed one thought at a time. The Bible says that the carnal mind is not subject to God—it is in fact enmity with God (Romans 8:7).

The tool we use to get our heads on straight is the Word—both the written Word (Scripture) and the living Word (Christ). It's up to us how well this process goes. Some people have incredible born-again experiences but do not pursue renewing their minds. Their old ways of thinking fight everything God is trying to accomplish in their lives.

So any thinking that is not exposed to light is dark. The Word is like the ultimate light bulb: when it turns on, the darkness departs. We are called from darkness to light—from ignorance to truth-knowledge. Jesus said that we would know the truth and the truth would set us free (John 8:32). There you have it: knowing is what brings freedom from the Enemy's lies and nonsense—from darkness.

A stronghold of darkness is established when you believe a lie to be a truth. A stronghold needs to be overcome:

> For though we walk in the flesh, we do not war according to the flesh.
> For the weapons of our warfare are not carnal but mighty in God for
> pulling down strongholds, casting down arguments and every high thing
> that exalts itself against the knowledge of God, bringing every thought
> into captivity to the obedience of Christ. (2 Corinthians 10:3–5)

That's the goal: to get our thinking full of the knowledge of God. In any area of life where we don't know the Word of God, we're vulnerable to enemy activity. That's why I say, *The only place the Enemy can travel is between your ears.*

I ask people who come to me with a life that's messed up in one way or another, "How did you think your way here?"

Wherever your life is going, you get there "head" first.

But the great thing about thinking is that you can change your life anytime you want to by changing your thinking!

Our problem today is that we like to depend on our own knowledge. We're a generation of know-it-alls who rebel against parents, law enforcement, and any other authority that's been put in our lives to help us.

When God created you, He didn't intend for you to have to learn by trial and error. He is constantly trying to show you that there's an easier way to live life than for you to have to constantly screw up in order to advance.

In the first place, we have the inspired Word of God to read and follow. On top of that we have our built-in internal guide, the Holy Spirit, who will help us be smart and not stupid. Jesus promised:

The Helper, the Holy Spirit, whom the Father will send in My name, He will teach you all things, and bring to your remembrance all things that I said to you. (John 14:26)

When you have that Person sharing good advice with you 24/7, there's no need to wear a dunce cap when making decisions and choices.

WEAPON 8: PRIDE

This is a weapon that the Enemy uses constantly.

The story of Naaman, the successful military man with the incurable disease of leprosy (2 Kings 5:1–19), reveals many facets of the human situation—one being pride.

Naaman had to humble himself several times before he got the healing he needed. First, Naaman had to receive and act on the advice of a servant girl. You can imagine what a pill that was to swallow in an ancient culture. A general taking advice from a *girl*? Next, Naaman had to visit Elisha, and the prophet didn't even meet with him in person. Naaman was offended and became furious. Then Elisha's instructions to Naaman to go dunk himself seven times in the filthy Jordan River also made Naaman angry.

Elisha, though, knew what was required of Naaman: the pride had to be rinsed out of Naaman's life so that God could do something exceptional.

Naaman was desperate, so he humbled himself. And God did something exceptional. Naaman came up out of the water with skin like a baby's—healed! More than that, God had removed pride and importance from Naaman, along with his leprosy.

Now a humbled Naaman could give thanks and praise God.

Does God want to make you an exception? Do you want to lead an exceptional life? Do you want to be unique in your own right? You must embrace this truth:

The desire for importance can be
the enemy of significance.

Maybe God needs to deal with pride on the inside of you before He can bring healing and restore an area of your life. Maybe you're in an internal struggle that you have learned to live with that God doesn't want you to live with.

If you can humble yourself and remove pride from the places in your life that don't work right, they can be brought to life.

There's one weapon you possess that has the firepower to knock out pride every time: *humility.*

WEAPON 9: FAMILIARITY

When our church was still small and didn't have a pastoral staff, my wife, Hope, and I would personally go to family court to offer support to church members struggling through big life issues, usually divorce.

Family court is one of the most horrible places I have ever been. Here, opposing lawyers take apart a man and a woman. Everything this couple ever lived through—all the dirt, all the secrets, all the shame—is thrown out on the table. It helps you understand why divorce is so incredibly painful and destructive, because these are two people who gave each other most of that information inside a covenant in which they vowed to protect each other. Now each one is thinking, *The information I gave you while you covered me is the same information you're using as ammunition to win the prizes: our kids and our stuff.*

This was the man whose call she had to get before she could go to sleep. This was the woman whose perfume sent him to seventh heaven. But whereas once they couldn't keep their hands off each other, now lawyers are trying to keep them from putting their hands around each other's necks!

Hope and I would sit there watching these people having their guts ripped out, and we'd weep. What went wrong? How did something so beautiful become so hideous? I'll tell you what happened: at some point they learned everything about each other, and they weren't equipped to handle it with honor and respect.

It certainly does not need to be this way, but I'm afraid too often...

Familiarity destroys honor.

Listen carefully, because this can change your marriage: The root word of *familiarity* is *family*. And I have found that it's usually in the family relationship, in the closest relationships in our lives, in our own house, where there is no honor. Why? Because I now know everything that's wrong with you. Sure, I honored you while we were dating, but that was before I ever heard you blow your nose in the shower. That was before I saw you leave your dirty dishes on the table. That was before you went to the bathroom with the door open. Now I've become significantly familiar with you, and now, without intentional focus on keeping honor, I am beginning to see all your flaws, all the things I didn't picture in my "dream life."

The honor begins to seep away and familiarity sets in.

Why could Jesus do no miracles in Nazareth? And why couldn't He be received in His own hometown as the Messiah? Everything that the Old Testament prophets had foretold, and everything that every Jew had ever longed for, was standing before them, but they couldn't receive Him (Mark 6:1–6). The familiarity of being around Jesus for upward of thirty years destroyed the honor God had placed on His life. They were too familiar with seeing Him as a carpenter's son.

What a shame if our marriages or other close relationships begin to become places where God can't do the miraculous, move mountains, change the unchangeable, perform the unexpected, heal, restore, and give life to dead things, simply because we've become too familiar with each other. The Enemy will use this to destroy people. Thankfully, restoring honor restores the opportunity for God to change things.

It's been said that familiarity breeds contempt, and there is a time when people have a tendency to turn on the people who used to be a blessing to them. I heard author Dr. Myles Munroe say it well: "It's the nature of people to turn on what used to turn them on."

WEAPON 10: BAD THINKING

Most of your battles in life will be determined by how you think and by your mind-set.

Two striking scriptures give us a picture of how thinking can affect our ability to fight and win.

Forever, O LORD, Your word is settled in heaven. (Psalm 119:89)

Lay aside all filthiness and overflow of wickedness, and receive
with meekness the implanted word, which is able to save your
souls. (James 1:21)

In other words, God is telling us that the only word that changes things is the word that sticks with us.

Bad thinking that sticks will take our lives in the opposite direction of God's plan for us. Bad thinking is a weapon we must constantly battle as new situations in life bring opportunities to choose between believing what we hear from darkness and believing God's promises about us.

Remember as a child, when your parents perhaps said to you, "You can do anything you want to if you set your mind to it"? Do you have a mind set on what God desires? Let me explain this as a critical principle, not just spiritual verbiage you may be accustomed to hearing all the time.

When the Bible instructs us, "Set your mind on things above, not on things on the earth" (Colossians 3:2), that word *set* refers to setting a bone that's been broken. I played a lot of sports growing up, and I'm a pretty active guy, so unfortunately I'm an authority on the subject of broken bones—I've had thirteen of them. In fact, I've spent three and a half years of my life in some form of cast! I don't recommend it.

Here's a fascinating fact, though: when a bone is set, it heals stronger than it previously was.

This principle works in other applications as well:

God cannot "set" your mind until it's been broken from the way it used to think.

I can't give you new information until you're willing to separate yourself from old information, which is why God said you can't put new wine into an old wineskin (Luke 5:37). The new wine will conflict with the very fiber of the old wineskin and eat it away.

The Word of God never works inside you until it's set, and set appropriately. The psalmist said, "Your word is *settled* in heaven" (119:89, emphasis added). It's that same word *set*.

And just as God's Word has been settled in heaven, so it has to be settled in your heart. What does that mean? It means it's been put in place, and it's healed stronger than your previous mind-set. You don't think the old way anymore because you have a new thinking that replaced your old thought paradigm.

I was fascinated to learn from a neurologist one day that the grooves in our brains are thinking patterns. In other words, how you think actually affects the structure of your brain! This neurologist also told me that it's possible for people to rewrite the grooves in their brains if they will accept new patterns of thinking. Your brain, literally and physically, will change in shape and contour if you can release old information and fill your mind with the knowledge of God.

Amazing! Good thinking doesn't just change the perception of things; it actually changes the physical mechanism of the brain.

Now I see that there's more to this "renewing of your mind" (Romans 12:2) than I realized.

—

The Enemy of our souls has many weapons that can do us in. But it can happen only if we drop the protection provided us by the One who has defeated every foe on our behalf:

> He has delivered us from the power of darkness and conveyed us into the kingdom of the Son of His love. (Colossians 1:13)

PART 6

PROWLING YOUR NEIGHBORHOOD

When our enemy really plays dirty, he attacks close to home.

If he can mess with your spouse or your kids, he's got a noose around your neck—and he'll take you out if you don't know how to wage the fight.

Is overcoming these family challenges really necessary to advance God's purposes?

Certainly our family members or others close to us are not *the* Enemy, but since he has no scruples and operates out of perfect hate, you will definitely see his influence in your "neighborhood." Remember what Peter said—"Stay alert! Watch out for your great enemy, the devil. He prowls around like a roaring lion, looking for someone to devour" (1 Peter 5:8, NLT).

When I went through the crisis related to the single moms' program, my entire family came under horrific attack. Although I certainly had made some mistakes with priorities and boundaries over the years, the ministry had never been my mistress. I had made the ministry take a backseat to my family, no matter how great the demands were. But with the mess that came upon us, there was no way to insulate my wife and kids from the storm of criticism and accusations I was receiving in the media. Every time my face came through a door, I met microphones and TV cameras. It was a nightmare.

The perception among the public was that somehow I had wronged the most vulnerable people of our community. This stirred great anger against me, and threatening messages started coming in through our home phone and the switchboard at church. People (who of course did not leave a number where we could reach them) called to say things like, "Carpenter, you're a scumbag and need to fold up and leave town. How dare you take money from these single moms?" Some callers threatened to harm me and my family, so during the worst of the news barrage, the ministry paid for twenty-four-hour security.

We went from being a normal family that did all the things families do, to living like soldiers in foxholes pinned down by enemy fire. Our house became a fortress—for security reasons, we had a fence built around our property. At night I would turn off the lights in the house and look out the window, where a police cruiser was parked in the driveway, protecting our safety.

Now we had to plan ahead where we would go and when. Every time I stepped out of my house, I had to confront what was going on. Every restaurant I went to, every gas line I stood in, every mall I shopped in required an ongoing defense of myself. This was not the way my wife and children—nor I—wanted to live.

Hope was nearly smashed by the pressure. Her personality had always been so bubbly and outgoing. She lived by adventure, was the life of the party, and now we were walled off. Old friends starting avoiding us; we had become "awkward."

Hope slowly slid into a depression that hung on a long time and altered her personality. At times she would not get out of bed for days. We had given everything we had in our adult lives to a community, and then almost overnight we saw that community alienated from us. It was devastating to both of us, but I think I endured it better than Hope. She just was not built to take the same kind of beating I was.

The kids were totally bewildered. It wasn't just the reproach of me being their dad, but they faced persecution at school. We kept moving them around to find a school where the hazing would subside and they could be treated like any other kids. But the whispers and the rolling of eyes and the passing of notes and the jokes kept coming.

One of the most wounding experiences came right before one Christmas. We needed to do some shopping, but Hope, worn out by the ordeal, stayed home. I took our three kids to the mall, and one after another, people swore at me and said hateful things. The children just looked at me and asked, "Why are they doing that, Dad?"

That really hurt. I mumbled an answer that didn't say much. How do you explain heckling to small children? They just wanted to be kids. They didn't care if they were so-and-so's child or a TV preacher's little celebrities. They simply wanted a dad. And what I was going through—the enemy I was fighting and the adversity I was facing—would not let me just be Dad.

Maybe the worst was that one of our kids, in grade school at the time, began to struggle with anxiety issues. He had to be heavily medicated, and we ended up having to homeschool him for six years. This ripped my heart out of my chest.

The fabric of my family was coming apart, and I had always been a family man trying to tend to my fatherly and husbandly responsibilities as God would expect me to. At times I didn't know if I would even be able to hold my family together.

I suppose I'm a fairly tough, resilient guy who does not let many things affect him. But with my family, the Enemy had found a vulnerable spot. I was ready to give up. *How could God use this trial to move me closer to His purposes for our family and my life?*

One thing was for sure—the enemy was not my marriage or my family. As you might expect, the situation we faced was very difficult for Hope and me. It can happen that when a family has unusual stress, such as we were facing in the ministry and with our kids, a couple will turn on each other. We certainly struggled at times, but we continued to cling to each other. It's important, in a discussion of the necessity of an enemy, that we not get confused about something: some relationships do come and go, but not so with covenant relationships.

Covenant relationships were meant for you to work together against whatever enemy is attacking that covenant.

I want to be blunt here: Do not think that your husband or wife is an enemy that you need to defeat or discard in order to achieve God's purpose for your life! Marriage is a covenant relationship. A covenant relationship is one that God means to go the distance.

Marriage can be a tough deal, but trust me, your husband or wife is not the enemy! I know—sometimes it feels that way. But the way we are asked to love our spouses goes beyond feelings and challenges. We don't discard our spouses as soon as they become annoying or feel like drags on our lives.

Enemies may try to destroy a relationship that God wants sustained, but you don't get rid of the spouse; you get rid of the enemy that's trying to tear the two of you apart. You take the giants that want to destroy your marriage, and you bring them to the forefront, discuss them, and deal with them.

Here's an example of how this might play out: We know from the Bible that God appoints the husband as the priest of the home—he's accountable for the order of the home and the vision that is cast for the family. Let's say a husband really feels like God is making a way to break a curse of poverty that has plagued the man's family for generations. This guy works hard and is beginning to see financial blessings. He maneuvers himself to a point where he is making wise decisions that are leading his family toward financial freedom. But his wife struggles with impulsive spending, which is threatening the financial health of the family.

The enemy in this case is not the wife. If the husband were to say, "Well, to secure our family financially, I need to get rid of her!" that would be a total misinterpretation of the principles taught in this book. The problem—the enemy—here is the lack of control and discipline concerning finances, revealed by the wife's careless spending. Together, as part of their covenant to honor each other, the husband and wife need to confront the problem and work on it.

I know, that's easier said than done, but life here on earth ain't about easy!

WHICH WINDOW IS OPEN?

efore I say much more about how to deal with enemies that appear too close to home, I want to review some basic facts about people.

For example, have you noticed how fickle we human beings are? One moment we are showering love and blessing on others. Then in a flash we can become like Hitler—little dictators ready to destroy with our words or actions even people we love dearly. It's not a pretty picture.

In life we can be cooperating with what God wants and letting in blessings to others via what I like to call the "windows of heaven." Or just the opposite, we can quickly become the "windows of hell" and release all kinds of misery into the earth. Am I punching any of your buttons on this? You can be in church praising God, and you're the windows of heaven, releasing glory into the building. Less than thirty minutes later, you can be out of church and in a restaurant with your family when a waitress spills tea in your lap. *Bam!* You lose your temper and give her some stinging words. Just like that, you've become a gateway of hell into this earth and into someone's life. It's that easy. It happens that fast.

Let's look more closely at the biblical example of this that I used back in the beginning of this book.

When Jesus came into the region of Caesarea Philippi, He asked His disciples, saying, "Who do men say that I, the Son of Man, am?"

So they said, "Some say John the Baptist, some Elijah, and others Jeremiah or one of the prophets."

He said to them, "But who do you say that I am?"

Simon Peter answered and said, "You are the Christ, the Son of the living God."

Jesus answered and said to him, "Blessed are you, Simon Bar-Jonah, for flesh and blood has not revealed this to you, but My Father who is in heaven."…

From that time Jesus began to show to His disciples that He must go to Jerusalem, and suffer many things from the elders and chief priests and scribes, and be killed, and be raised the third day.

Then Peter took Him aside and began to rebuke Him, saying, "Far be it from You, Lord; this shall not happen to You!"

But He turned and said to Peter, "Get behind Me, Satan! You are an offense to Me, for you are not mindful of the things of God, but the things of men." (Matthew 16:13–17, 21–23)

What we are seeing here is fascinating in the context of recognizing enemies working through people. One minute Peter is hearing from heaven, and the next minute he's standing in the way of Jesus's destiny! So Jesus, seeing the truth of what's really happening, says, "Get behind Me, Satan!" He isn't speaking to Peter; He is speaking to the Enemy He sees working through Peter.

In other words, Jesus is saying, "Peter, you are being used to stop me from my purpose right now, because you have in mind the things of man and of the Enemy, not the purpose of God for my life." Straight from the windows of heaven to the gates of hell.

I know all about this from personal experience.

I've heard many times how, on the way to church on Sunday, Mama and Daddy aren't talking, and the kids in the backseat may have on clean clothes but their attitude smells bad. Well, let me tell you, it happens in the pastor's car too.

I remember one Sunday when the Lord gave me some fresh insights that I delivered with great passion to my congregation. Oh, they loved it—I floated out of there with the handclaps still ringing in my ears.

We were driving home after the service when another driver cut me off on the highway. I got instantly mad. I started bashing the other driver verbally, waving my arms around—face red, spit flying. Hope looked over at me and said, "Hey, preacher man, what happened to you since you gave your talk?"

Ouch. Yup, that windows-of-heaven or windows-of-hell deal applies to all of us.

THE NATURE-OF-PEOPLE PRINCIPLE

While teaching years ago, Dr. Myles Munroe shared one sentence that shifted my thinking forever. The basic premise was this:

The nature of a thing determines the behavior and performance of a thing.

I think this is brilliant! I have built from this idea a concept I call the nature-of-people principle. Learning this idea will help you recognize your enemies and know how to prepare for battle with them. And, maybe even more important, it will help you identify which friendships will be critical to have in your life.

Here are some examples of how the nature-of-people principle works in real life: If a woman understands that her husband likes peace at home, she shouldn't be surprised if he withdraws from conflict. If a man knows that his wife longs for security, he shouldn't be surprised if she's unsettled when he changes jobs every six months. These same kinds of things apply with teenagers, parents, bosses, and most people you find yourself in relationship with.

So a key to interpreting behavior is to understand a person's nature. To understand this principle better, think about a Corvette. This powerful sports car will operate according to its nature: don't expect great gas mileage, and it won't haul a family of six. However, it will snap your neck by going from zero to sixty in four seconds and, with its convertible top down, give you a fun day in the sun with your sweetheart or a friend.

The Corvette acts according to its nature. People do the same.

When we ignore the nature-of-people principle, we often end up disappointed. Here's why:

**Anywhere there's disappointment, you'll find a
root of false expectations for something to
produce what it was not designed to produce.**

In fact, anytime there is conflict in a relationship, you'll discover this principle is at work, and you'll find resentment, anger, mistrust, disappointment, and many other emotions, all stemming from a false expectation either unarticulated or unrealistically set. In other words, someone is expecting something that goes against the grain of the other person's nature.

Of course, human sin is always in the mix too. People are more complicated than cars. A car does not have a will of its own; it can't decide one day that it would rather be a bus than a Corvette. People, however, can make all kinds of choices that go beyond their basic nature.

One more piece of related advice could save you many fruitless "discussions" with the people you love:

Conflict is the gap between expectations and reality.

(That was a bonus I threw in because on page 133 you are still reading my book!)

LOVE AND WAR WITH THE SAME ENEMY

Didn't Jesus ask us to love our enemies? How does that work out, especially when someone we are close to is acting like an enemy?

In this book I'm not advocating doing any harm to or using violence against anyone—any conduct unbecoming to a follower of Christ. I *am* saying that while I may love someone, or love his or her soul dearly, that person can still become a great hindrance to where God has me going in life.

Jesus did say, "Do not think that I came to bring peace on earth. I did not come to bring peace but a sword. For I have come to 'set a man against his father, a daughter against her mother, and a daughter-in-law against her mother-in-law'; and 'a man's enemies will be those of his own household'" (Matthew 10:34–36).

Of course Jesus wasn't advocating that you not love your family, but He wanted you to understand that even those you love dearly may not agree with what God is doing in your life. Even His family gave Jesus grief (Mark 3:21). We know He loved them, but there was something more important going on than family relationships.

What Jesus said is pretty pointed: "A man's enemies will be those of his own household." Those are very close relationships. Your grandma may be as sweet as cherry pie, but she can be a stumbling block to what God wants you to do—and she probably doesn't realize it.

Proverbs 18:21 makes it clear that life and death both lie in the power of the tongue. All throughout the Scriptures, in fact, God talks to us about the power our words have in creating life and speaking to things to move, to live, to happen.

I believe it's critical for you to grasp this concept when you read about the scene at the foot of the cross, from perhaps a different perspective than you're used to. There's John, alongside Jesus's momma, and she's crying, wanting Him to live, calling His name (see John 19:25-26). It's completely understandable (especially for those of us who are parents) how in an emotional state she probably cried out for His life.

What I believe is also happening here, though, gives amazing insight into how the Enemy can use a scriptural principle and work through people to attempt to stop you from fulfilling your purpose.

Why did Jesus speak to John and instruct him to remove His mom? I believe that He had to, because He couldn't violate God's word, and God's word is clear: Whatever you speak to, you give life to. She, at this moment, is the last thing in the way of Jesus fulfilling His purpose. He was born to die, and her words were speaking life to Him.

I believe He was saying, "Go home. As long as your words bring life into this situation, I can't fulfill My purpose and die. Right now you aren't intentionally evil—you love Me. But you are an enemy to My purpose."

Mary's words, in effect, are carrying God's power into a situation that is not set up to receive it. This was supposed to be a time set aside for Him to die. There's nobody in my family whom I don't love. But I cannot allow them to cause me to forfeit something God has for me just because they don't agree with it. When God has something He intends for you, He doesn't go around and seek agreement from everybody who is tied to you before He'll bring it to pass. When you know you are walking in His purpose, you have to walk by faith and move forward, no matter how it makes other people feel.

It's the same way with you and me. There are many people we love, but they can become enemies to our purpose. We need to lovingly take care of them but resolutely continue on the path God has asked us to walk.

WATCH OUT FOR WOLVES

If you are operating in His love, even in very difficult relationships God has your back!

But the truth is that some people are just not good for us to hang out with.

Does that sound too harsh? If they're feeding the thing that wants to destroy you, they've chosen to align themselves with an enemy. Or if you're trying to get out of a promiscuous lifestyle and someone tries to lure you to that way of life again, if you hear that person's voice on your voice mail, hit Delete. Remember:

An enemy is someone who increases, strengthens, encourages, or enables an area of weakness in you that God wants to remove from your life.

Jesus warned us about the environment we live in: "Behold, I send you out as sheep in the midst of wolves" (Matthew 10:16). He was saying in so many words, "I'm sending you out among people who want to prey on you. I'm sending you into a world that's wrong where I'm expecting you to try to act right. I'm sending you into a world that cheats, and I'm asking you to walk in integrity. I'm sending you into a world that lies, and I'm commanding you to tell the truth."

In such a world, we are to be "wise as serpents and harmless as doves" (Matthew 10:16). The wisdom in love is not giving yourself away to everybody who comes across your path. In other words, be smart about starting and keeping relationships, and don't be led by your emotions.

Let's say you've got an addict in your family. When you don't enable her, she might say something like, "Well, I thought you loved me!"

Your smart response? "I do love you. That's why I'm not giving you more money, because you're taking it and buying drugs."

Not everyone in the world means you well, and not everybody out there is excited about your promotion and celebrating your success. You've got to understand who deserves to be in your life and who does not and where to draw boundaries.

Let's look further at what Jesus said when He portrayed us as wolf-encircled sheep:

> Beware of men, for they will deliver you up to councils and scourge you
> in their synagogues. You will be brought before governors and kings for
> My sake, as a testimony to them and to the Gentiles.... And you will
> be hated by all for My name's sake. But he who endures to the end
> will be saved. When they persecute you in this city, flee to another. For
> assuredly, I say to you, you will not have gone through the cities of Israel
> before the Son of Man comes.
>
> A disciple is not above his teacher, nor a servant above his master. It
> is enough for a disciple that he be like his teacher, and a servant like his
> master. If they have called the master of the house Beelzebub, how much
> more will they call those of his household! Therefore do not fear them.
> For there is nothing covered that will not be revealed, and hidden that
> will not be known. (Matthew 10:17–18, 22–26)

Jesus admonishes us to be wise, and then He starts listing betrayals and all the people who are going to come against us, because we'll need to discern who are friends and who are wolves.

Most of the time, to really hurt you, an enemy has to get close to you. This is important to recognize, because many times an enemy may disguise himself as a friend. Jesus referred to this as a wolf in sheep's clothing. This is when someone has an agenda but presents himself in a different way to get access to your world and your decisions.

The book of James says, "Where envy and self-seeking exist, confusion and every evil thing are there" (3:16). Self-seeking—that's what "wolves" are all about. If someone has an ambition for an outcome that benefits him regardless of the impact on you, others, and God, that's self-seeking. He has a desire, and he's determined to find a way to satisfy it.

The Bible says that wherever that attitude exists, so will every kind of evil, sin, lie, and carnality. Because when selfish ambition takes over, all bets are off.

So the wolf says, "I've come to aid the flock." But inside, the wolf is thinking, *As soon as I get in the flock, I'm going to take advantage of it and use it to serve my selfish ambitions.*

The advantage you have is that the Good Shepherd knows how to take care of His sheep.

THE JUDAS PROBLEM

There's another relational challenge we need to consider. You see, occasionally there's a "Judas" near you who looks like a friend but who is actually like a double agent working for the Enemy.

As I wrote at the beginning of the book, God can use a Judas, too, to advance you toward your purpose—as He did with Jesus. But you need to understand how a Judas operates.

In Luke 22:2 we learn that it was the chief priests and scribes who wanted to kill Jesus. Then, in the next verse, we read that Satan entered Judas, one of Jesus's twelve disciples. Judas, of course, would go on to betray Jesus, leading directly to the Lord's death.

This pattern is critical to understand, because if it happened to Jesus, it can happen to you.

A Judas is someone who is close to you and who has an agreement with someone else who wants to harm you.

Many people read the Bible and make the understandable argument that Judas was an enemy in Jesus's inner circle. However, I don't believe Judas was Jesus's primary enemy. The problem with Judas was that he embraced Jesus's enemies.

Whenever you have someone close to you who embraces your enemies, that relationship has the potential to become hazardous. A Judas is not only close by but can also weaken you through connection to others. A Judas gives an ear to your critics.

Judas did nothing directly to Jesus to harm Him, but he befriended the people who did.

Jesus said that a "house divided against itself will not stand" (Matthew 12:25). When we think of division, we think of one good guy and one bad guy. Actually, in many cases, that's not true. The word *division* simply means you have two *(di)* visions in the same house. Whether one person is good or bad doesn't matter that much. Two visions can't survive indefinitely because people will eventually cling to one and hate the other.

Remember Sarah and Hagar? They had two visions in the same house until Sarah made it clear: "She needs to leave" (Genesis 21).

Delilah was not Samson's enemy. She was Samson's Judas. His enemy was the Philistines, and Delilah revealed who the enemy was to Samson (Judges 16).

When the devil has come to the conclusion that he can't take you down from the outside, he seeks out somebody who can destroy you from within. Got a Judas in your life?

A BAD YOKE

Another effective enemy tactic is "unequal yoking."

When the Bible talks about an unequal yoking, it means a lot more than that you shouldn't marry somebody who isn't saved (2 Corinthians 6:14–7:1). When you have any kind of association with someone where there is inequity, where the other person is not going where you're going and doesn't see what you see, that's unequal yoking. You may find yourself so tied to someone else that you won't make a progressive decision without his or her agreement. The danger is that the other person is never going to agree with you, because the two of you are unequally yoked. You are sabotaging your future because you are yoked with someone who has a heart and purpose that differ from yours.

The book of Ezra tells the story of Zerubbabel, one of the key figures in rebuilding the Lord's temple. When some people showed up claiming to want to help with the building project, Zerubbabel had the wisdom to recognize that these people actually were enemies. Zerubbabel told them, "You may do nothing with us" (4:3).

No matter what your circumstances, it would be better to be by yourself than to tie yourself to the wrong people. Be on guard for relationships that represent an unequal yoking.

THE THREE COURTS OF INTIMACY

What is intimacy?

The word conjures up different things in different people's minds. Most people associate intimacy with physical or sexual experiences. However, after more than twenty years of pastoring and helping married couples in counseling, I can assure you that while intimacy includes those things, you can be physically and sexually active and still not have intimacy—it happens every day.

Our society has somehow embraced the notion that intimacy equals sex, but nothing could be further from the truth.

Intimacy is information. Intimacy in a relationship is created when we share things that are private and personal, deep secrets, with a certain person that we wouldn't share with another. That's why divorces and breakups are so devastatingly painful, because what was shared privately for the unselfish purpose of loving and creating intimacy ends up getting exposed publicly for personal gain.

When Jesus was concluding His earthly ministry, He said to His close followers: "No longer do I call you servants, for a servant does not know what his master is doing; but I have called you friends, for all things that I heard from My Father I have made known to you" (John 15:15).

Jesus was telling them that the nature of their relationship was about to change, and it was going to become much more intimate. The relationship wasn't going to be closer simply because they were going to spend more time together or share more common experiences. Instead, He was going to share more information directly with them than with anyone else; and the fact that they would have this information about Jesus and the Father—while others wouldn't—was going to make them more intimate.

Intimacy is "insider" knowledge, and it needs to be earned.

How, then, do we love others intimately and not let an enemy get close enough to destroy our purpose? Here's an example.

Whenever I get the opportunity to speak at singles' conferences, I tell my listeners that I know they feel as if their biological clocks are ticking. They find themselves at age twenty-seven, they've never been married, and they are desperate to find the "right one."

I explain to them the real problem: You've got to date long enough to see your partner in every season of life. You need to see him or her long enough to know what it's like to be with that person when things are going well and when they're not going so well. How does he respond when he loses his job? How does she treat you in front of her family and friends? How does he communicate with you when he has a stomach virus and is stuck in the bathroom for three days? How does she act when you have to go out of town on an unanticipated trip for work?

Don't let feeling lonely tie you up in a relationship knot that you can't untie just because you think it's better than being alone and feeling the blues.

Too many people date someone three or four times, and all of a sudden they're sitting in Starbucks telling the other person about past relationships, maybe even the past divorce. The other person has not earned that depth of information yet. That's called intimacy.

In a relationship, as you move from your first date to marriage, there are three levels: an outer court, an inner court, and then what I refer to as the holy of holies. By the inner court, I mean people who go way beyond the layer of "acquaintance" in your life. The inner court does not include someone you just met. It is someone you probably spend a lot of time with. These are the individuals you'd call close friends, who you might even invite to Christmas and birthday parties. However, they don't know the intimate details of your life and your struggles.

I observe it every day: people give sensitive things away to others who haven't yet earned it.

Start with the outer court. Only gradually move to the inner court, a place of more intimate but still cautious sharing.

The third level, the holy of holies, is reserved for the person you're called to be in covenant with. That's where you know her flaws, you know his weaknesses, you know her hurts, you know his experiences, and you've felt each other's pain. But before you get there, you need to have seen how each other responds during several seasons of life.

Trouble tends to come with scenarios like these:

- You worked together for three weeks and jumped into a business partnership.
- You met a woman at church, hit it off, and decided on the spot to let her be a full-time sitter for your children.
- You met a guy at the church singles' group on Wednesday night and decided to take a road trip with him the next weekend.

We know how powerful—and good—emotions are, but we can't allow them to drive fast decisions in any relationship. You can quickly set yourself up to find out later that an enemy has infiltrated the inner circle of your life.

Jesus wants you to tap into God's wisdom with the help of the Holy Spirit and not forget that when it comes to relationships, this is still enemy territory.

RELATIONSHIPS FOR REASONS AND SEASONS

Out of a genuine misunderstanding of the role of people in our lives, we sometimes create our own enemies. We begin to connect with someone around a project, an opportunity, a need, or a desire, but one or both of the people in the relationship misunderstand the purpose of the relationship and overstay their assignment.

This is a dangerous place to be, because, if you're not careful, you will create an enemy that God never intended for you to have out of a relationship that was supposed to be a blessing to both of you. That's when, if you're in any kind of leadership capacity, whether in your home, your ministry, your church, or a business, people begin to turn against you and move to disliking or even despising you.

So carefully, prayerfully evaluate the purpose of your relationships with this in mind:

Your inability to discern the role of certain relationships in your life will create enemies.

Have you ever had people who you at one time thought were with you, only to see them abandon you later? Of course you have. Most of us, at one time or another, have had to weather difficulties with relationships that turned stormy. Part of the problem stems from the false belief that everyone assigned to your life is assigned to it for a lifetime. Not true. In fact, I believe there are three categories of people who will come into your life at various points in your journey:

- people assigned for a reason
- people assigned for a season
- people (only a few) assigned for a lifetime

Even Jesus had to navigate difficult relationships.

Jesus had a peculiar relationship with John the Baptist. Remember, this was the same John who called Jesus out as the Son of God, who pointed Him out in ministry, who baptized Him, who was there when the Holy Spirit descended on Jesus like a dove and God expressed His pleasure with His "beloved Son" (Matthew 3:17). John respected Jesus immensely. But early on, when they spent time together in the wilderness, it was John—not Jesus—who was the leader of the big ministry.

Then later the relationship suddenly changes.

John is in prison, and when Jesus sends someone else instead of going to John Himself, John gets offended. Now John has no crowds, he's in prison, and Jesus is the one with all the buzz, the one who has to almost hide just to rest and to pray. John wants the old times, but Jesus sends a message to tell him that "the blind see, the lame walk, the lepers are cleansed, the deaf hear, the dead are raised, the poor have the gospel preached to them. And blessed is he who is not offended because of Me" (Luke 7:22–23).

Jesus is saying something that more than two thousand years later many others are still experiencing as they pursue their dreams and ascend to success: people are offended because the seasons of our lives change, and "I can't be to you who I used to be to you."

The key is learning to proactively manage the ups and downs of relationships and the comings and goings of people, always understanding that some people are meant to be a part of your life forever, while others are meant to be a part of your life temporarily.

I heard Bishop T. D. Jakes give the illustration that some people in your life will be like the building, and others will be like the scaffolding. The building is something that's made of cement and stone. It does not move and will be there for the long haul. Scaffolding is erected to help construct the building. There are some people who will be there for a season to help you build your life—as you will help others in the same way. But once the building is built, the scaffolding is taken down and put to use somewhere else.

The sooner you realize this, the less pain you'll have and the less time you'll spend grieving over a lost relationship. It is the ebb and flow of life, and it's the nature of people.

GUARD YOUR INVESTMENT IN DESTINY

I believe that with every generation a blessing and a cursing can gain momentum.

In Exodus 20 we learn that an iniquity can curse a bloodline as deep as four generations. I believe this means that what one generation may struggle with privately can become full blown in the next generation. However, I also believe that a blessing can increase from one generation to another.

We know that God changed Jacob's name to Israel, which means "prince." But Israel never became a prince. It was his son Joseph who became a prince. Here we have a blessing gaining momentum for future generations.

And because there was such a great call on Joseph's life, is it any wonder that enemies lurked around every corner, trying to sabotage his future? From being rejected by his brothers, lied about, sold as a slave, thrown into prison, accused of immorality, and so much more, his life reveals how well the Enemy knew from the onset that greatness was locked up in this man.

The level of difficulty you face in battle is an indicator of the greatness that is on your life and on future generations.

Small futures are birthed by small battles.

Great futures are birthed by great battles.

Could it be that your difficulty is only a sign of how wonderful your tomorrow could be?

Could it be that your enemy knows something you don't know about yourself?

Sometimes that's why battles are so difficult—because we see ourselves one way but the Enemy sees us another way.

Therefore I believe God raised me up to touch people whom my father never got a chance to touch. I also believe that God is raising our children up to touch people Hope and I will never touch and do things we will never get a chance to do.

This means the Enemy has a huge stake in messing up their lives, just as he wants to destroy us. Good, godly parenting goes beyond things like reading the right books and taking the kids to church. We need God's wisdom to help us navigate our role as parents. That means prayer—asking for wisdom, engaging in intercession, and hearing what the Holy Spirit says. One story will explain why I say this.

On a New Year's Eve a few years ago, I was awakened at one o'clock in the morning. Now, I am sure that our children are typical of most children in that they don't glow in the dark and sing, "Holy, holy, holy" all day long. We have many of the same struggles with raising kids as any other normal family. And on this particular night, our oldest son—a teenager at the time—was supposed to be at another person's house, but with his curfew already passed, he was still out with some friends. But we weren't aware of it.

I was awakened from a deep sleep and knew instantly that something was wrong. I grabbed Hope's hand and said, "We have to pray for our son now!" This startled and scared her, but she took my hand and, without getting up, we offered up a short prayer for God's protection over him.

At 1:15 a.m. our son had a car accident. He called us a few minutes later, and when I arrived at the scene after 2:00 a.m., I looked at where my son's car was and shook my head. He had spun wildly out of control, left the road, slid by a light pole and a tree in his path, and come to a stop perfectly in the only parking space where there was no car in an entire apartment complex. It looked like our son had parked the car in that space. Both he and the car escaped without a scratch.

I really believe that God woke me up fifteen minutes before that crash because there was an enemy wanting to stop a destiny from taking place.

Our younger son struggled with an unthinkable battle for most parents. For six long years, Hope and I battled every day as our son, at a very early age, found himself fighting severe anxiety attacks that gripped him with fear and pounded him daily. I promise you, this is one of the most gut-wrenching things for any parent to endure. Imagine six excruciating years, day after day, watching your baby boy gripped with this condition.

I would get on the floor with him, in tears, dripping with sweat while trying to calm him down long enough to whisper to him, each time, to remind him of the Word and show him how many others had fought and beat enemies before him. I reminded him day after day, attack after attack, month after month, year after year, "Son, the fact this is happening to you at such a young age is an indicator that there's something so great on the inside of you that it will crush the Enemy if it ever gets out. He knows that, and he wants to crush it before it crushes him."

That was my battle cry to my son.

We know destiny is so important because many times in the Bible, the Enemy knows someone's destiny is great, and he seeks to snuff it out when the person is young. Why else did the Enemy try to take Moses out as a child? Or Jesus? Why were the decrees made to kill all the babies? Why did we pray for our son the night of his crash? Why did we battle with our younger son against such a debilitating condition? Because the Enemy is after destiny. He may not be after you now, but he certainly is after everything God wants to do with your future. And with the future of your offspring.

PART 7

HOW TO FIGHT TO WIN

The darkness had about overwhelmed me when I saw a ray of light.

It happened right after Christmas in December 2007. After a long day in a room full of lawyers, I reached a settlement. I had decided to call off all the dogs and strike a deal on the class-action lawsuit against the church and me.

I'm a fighter—I hated "giving up." I had done nothing wrong, and I wanted my name cleared. I wanted to prove to everybody that my motives on the single moms' program had been pure and I had not been involved in any way with the scam. But my lawyer had told me earlier, "Pastor Carpenter, I think you're going to win in this lawsuit. You had the sign-off from the attorney general, and the church had done due diligence. The FBI and the South Carolina Law Enforcement Division ended their investigations—you're clean. But you are losing the battle in the media."

I hated to admit it, but I knew he was right. The public relations war being waged against me was crushing my family, our church, and me. The loyalty of some of my church staff was wobbling. Some splitting of the church was underway—that had never happened in our history—as people were grumbling and leaving. It was a horrible mess.

And so, facing the greatest defeat of my life, I submitted to my legal counsel and decided to settle the lawsuit and make peace with everybody I could—to stop the bloodletting.

After nine hours of painful deliberation on that winter day, all the parties made a deal. All allegations against me were dropped. My name was cleared, and I had my life back.

But at what cost?

I went home feeling more defeated and discouraged, more dead on the inside than I had ever felt. I had always believed the best in people, but I left that meeting not so sure about people anymore. I felt like everybody was a Judas. I had given my heart and poured my passion into so many for so long. Now, the way I felt, I wanted to say, "If that's what you get at the end of giving your life away, I want to keep my life to myself!"

I was a broken man. And since I was so isolated and without mentors and close friends, I had to claw my way through the darkness and pain by myself to try to find a reason to go on and make sense of all the tragedy.

The weight of it all really fell on me after the settlement. With the day-to-day battle over, I now had some time to reflect on how much it had damaged me, my wife, my kids, my church, everything.

I had never felt such disillusionment with ministry in my life. How would I respond? I knew I would have to drill down very deep spiritually to find the strength to go on.

And this was not the end of the pain. Shortly thereafter some key personnel at church resigned, leaving holes in the ministry. Some others on the staff—people who were precious to me—left and sought to start another church.

As I've explained in this book already, however, this is when my understanding was birthed of why God had allowed these things to happen. In my personal time alone with God, crying out to Him for comfort and understanding, I began to see things in the Bible that I had overlooked before. In case after case I found out that…

The viciousness of a battle is a clue to the greatness of the coming breakthrough.

A great enemy signals a great triumph.

Dwelling on these concepts, which I discovered throughout the Word of God, began to give me the hope to see that maybe, just maybe, these great enemies that I had faced had set me up for the biggest things that could ever happen in my life. In this period of darkness, I ran into the arms of God, soaked myself in the Word, and discovered the necessity of an enemy.

I saw that there was a plan and reasons, after all.

This book is the result.

Now, after sharing my story and many of the principles related to this topic, I want to give you some final tips to help you win your battle.

FAITH IN GOD AND HIS PLAN

Without faith it is impossible to please God (Hebrews 11:6). Not *hard* to please. Not hard to please *sometimes*. No, *impossible*—period. End of story.

This is the first element of a winning strategy—without faith in God, you are going to lose.

Faith does require something of us: When you hold a small seed in your hand, it takes faith to believe that the seed could someday be a tree that produces baskets of fruit. The Enemy sets up situations that look different from what you heard about them.

We are not to live by what we see, but your enemy for sure wants you to live by something that you saw, something that contradicted what God said about you or your situation, because even he knows that what's in you is always greater than what's around you.

The story of Peter walking on water is a well-documented example of such faith. Jesus stood on the water, and the disciples at first thought He was a ghost. Not sure he was recognizing Jesus, Peter shouted, "Lord, if it is You, command me to come to You on the water" (Matthew 14:28). Jesus responded by speaking one word: "Come." By faith, Peter got out of the boat and began to walk on the water.

Now I want to rattle your theological world a little: In spite of how it's been told by so many great preachers, I submit to you that Peter never walked on water—nor has anyone else! I'm not playing a semantic game; I believe there's a significant mind-set shift that needs to be made before you can see the power you have inside you, which this story about Peter documents.

It's impossible to walk on water, because water does not have the consistency to hold a man's weight unless it's frozen. That's why I propose this:

Peter did not walk on water. Peter walked on word.

In reality, had Jesus not spoken the word, there would have been nothing to sustain Peter while he was walking. When Jesus said the word "Come," everything Peter needed to get out of that boat and for a miracle to happen was available to hold him up. The word from Jesus came into the situation and, contrary to what it looked like conditionally, the word sustained Peter, and he "walked on water."

The miracle took place because of what Peter *heard*, because as we know, faith comes by "hearing...the word of God" (Romans 10:17). But when Peter *saw* the wind and the waves and began to focus on what he *saw*, and when he realized that what he saw contradicted what he *heard*, then like what most of us would have done, Peter put his faith in what he saw instead of what Jesus had spoken to him about his circumstances. Then he sank.

Here's the principle:

It's your enemy's role to create circumstances around you that challenge the faith inside you.

That's why it's so important that you let the Word of God create an image of faith inside you that is the reality you "see" so that you can face and overcome every enemy and every trial you face in life.

Right now, as you are reading this, you may be at a point in your career, your marriage, your finances, or another area of your life where it feels as if an enemy is destroying you. If that's your situation, I have great news for you: the presence of an enemy is telling you how available your future and calling still are!

Now it's up to you to engage that enemy, not based on what you are *seeing* in your circumstances, but based on the promises—the truth—of what you are *hearing* in the Word of God.

This hearing-versus-seeing conflict will happen regularly in your life. God will speak one thing to you, and the Enemy will show you something that contradicts it, because he is there to steal the seed. The potential lies inside you for greatness every day of your life, but the Enemy wants that greatness stopped.

This is why it's mandatory that you know who you are and what you possess *in Christ.* As a follower of Him, you have within you the same power that raised Jesus from the dead:

> And what is the exceeding greatness of His power toward us who believe, according to the working of His mighty power which He worked in Christ when He raised Him from the dead and seated Him at His right hand in the heavenly places. (Ephesians 1:19–20)

To defeat an enemy, you must hear what God says and act accordingly.

QUIET FAITH

I learned during this season of great battle that often, in the early stages of seeking God's purpose for your life, you'll have to defend your vision. The greatest way to silence your critics isn't to respond—that fuels them. Just keep doing what God told you to do.

This is the promise in God's Word:

> The *vision* is yet for an appointed time; but at the end it *will speak,* and
> it will not lie. Though it tarries, wait for it; because it will surely come,
> it will not tarry. (Habakkuk 2:3, emphasis added)

Once God gave me victory over these enemies, He moved me into a new day. I learned a valuable lesson through this:

In the beginning, you'll have to defend your vision.
But after you win, your vision will defend you.

Ultimately, your vision will speak for itself.

Although during my ordeal I did defend myself at times as the mud flew in my direction, mostly I kept my mouth shut. I tried to live with a quiet faith.

Often people think that faith is loud and boisterous—shouting down the devil and that kind of thing. But often the greatest faith is silent.

The supreme example of this was Jesus, who remained silent as accusations and questions were thrown at Him in the last hours before the Crucifixion (Matthew 26:62–63).

I don't think that the walls of Jericho fell because on the seventh day, on the seventh round trip, the people shouted so loud that a harmonic vibration disintegrated the walls (Hebrews 11:30). I think the walls fell because the people were able to walk around for the previous six days, keep their mouths shut, and quietly build faith in the ability of almighty God to act!

When the accusations flew at me, I never cursed my community. I never cursed the people who were cursing me. I tried to remain humble—and quiet. And I watched God ultimately vindicate me with the investigating agencies and the court system. I watched God remove the lawsuit—totally strike it from the record.

I watched the efforts of many who tried to destroy our name, and I watched our ministry fall apart. I did nothing and watched God totally, completely rescue and vindicate me. And then I watched God bring incredible changes in our congregation—just as one group of people was leaving, another group of people came in. The church survived and is stronger than ever.

So when the Enemy approaches, fall to your knees, declare your faith in God, submit to His plans, and keep quiet.

Then, as you see the walls falling, give Him the glory.

THE NUKES IN YOUR ARSENAL

As we enter every battle and fight against each enemy that threatens our purpose, God has equipped us with two significant weapons—mercy and grace.

These two are so unbelievably potent that I call them spiritual "nukes." And as each of us has different assignments on our lives, I believe we are given an appropriate measure of both of these weapons.

Understanding mercy and grace, and realizing the difference between the two, is a critical insight to grasp prior to adversity. Hebrews 4:16 says this: "Let us…come boldly to the throne of grace, that we may obtain mercy and find grace to help in time of need."

The Bible states that we are to come to *obtain* mercy but we *find* grace. Many Christians use mercy and grace interchangeably, but the two words are quite different. Here's a simple way to grasp the meaning of grace: grace is not when God stops something that should have happened; it's when God gives you something you don't deserve, and it can't be earned.

Notice that the Bible doesn't declare that we were saved by mercy. We were saved by grace, because grace is something God gave us that we did not deserve, and it cannot be earned. But when we come before God, according to the Bible, we *obtain* mercy. In other words, when we cry out for mercy, God gets between the blow and us. You and I can cry out to God, and He will immediately shield us from our Enemy and not allow us to get hit with the full weight of what the Enemy wants to bring against our lives.

However, the writer of Hebrews wrote that we have to find grace. I believe this means that grace is a journey. You have to go through a discovery process to find all the things that God has given. Grace is not obtained immediately; it develops. It happens over time as we grow in our walk with God.

So by summarizing several principles, we learn that

- God will give you the framework of your future by giving you a word;
- He will let you come into His presence to obtain mercy,
- but you have to find and grow in grace.

When an obvious enemy shows up, I know that because of God's *mercy* He will not allow anything to come against me that is more than I can bear. And, as I walk through the battle, I will never lack what I need to survive, and ultimately I will thrive because of His ever-fresh and growing supply of *grace*.

PICK YOUR BATTLES

Jesus was a very practical man, and His practical advice still holds today. He told us not to start things unless we intend to finish them (Luke 14:28–30). In other words, we can't do everything. We can't fight every battle.

As I have experienced increased responsibility and success in ministry, I have learned that I have to carefully pick my battles. Unfortunately, the reality of success is that the more of it you experience, the more battles you'll be asked to join. I've learned that very few, ultimately, are worth fighting because there aren't that many battles I was called to fight.

I remember a situation a few years ago that challenged but eventually confirmed this principle for me.

Scripture clearly commands us to honor those in authority over us in government. Therefore, as a church we've always allowed any elected official who requests to visit our congregation and worship with us to do just that, and we give him or her a few minutes prior to the service to address the congregation. We do have a few simple boundaries: they are not to campaign but are simply to share about themselves personally and their walk of faith.

Since we have a large congregation, when candidates for major offices are campaigning, they routinely call and want to make a visit to the church.

So we were not surprised when then-Senator Barack Obama, who was running for president, called and expressed interest in spending time with me, worshiping with us, and addressing our congregation. As per our policy, we welcomed him.

Following his visit (which of course was covered before and after in our local media), a caller made an unbelievably derogatory comment about me on a local radio talk show. The host said some things in an attempt to balance the discussion, but then others called in to lambaste me and the church.

My cell phone lit up immediately with staff members enraged, urging me to call the show to defend myself. Hope called as well, very unhappy with what had been said about me.

I chose to not respond because...

An enemy will let you swing away all day, and you accomplish nothing except wearing yourself out.

When King David was a boy, he privately practiced honing his skill with a sling. And eventually God saw that he was ready to display that gift publicly. So Goliath entered the picture, and a real, necessary battle ensued. I wonder, though, how many times David was taunted and tempted to fight a battle that wasn't the one God was preparing him for one day.

Think about this: if you're spending a lot of time swinging away, you'd better make sure it's preparing you for a battle worthy of your fight.

So, how do we choose the right battles? I have learned to ask myself two questions. First, are there spoils to be gained through victory in this battle? If there's nothing to be gained, I'm not going to fight. When I say "gained," I'm not talking about gaining the opinion of a caller on a radio show, because if I actually had managed to convince him that I'm not what he said I was, what have I really accomplished? At best, I've modified—maybe—the opinion of the caller and a few others, so that might make me feel better about myself and my reputation. Frankly, with all the pressing tasks on my plate, such an effort is not worth the time.

A spoil would be something that clearly spreads the gospel, honors Jesus, and advances the kingdom of God. In this case I chose not to call the radio show and get into a word fight with anonymous, angry callers.

I've decided that I'm not going to get up every morning and go to bed every night thinking about some enemy. What I do is get up every morning and go to bed every night thinking, *I wonder how big the prize is.*

The second question I ask when considering combat with an enemy is, does this situation threaten my destiny?

If something stands in the way of my future and purpose, I will engage it with everything I have, because I have a future; I have a hope; I have a purpose, an assignment, a destiny; and I am focused on finishing what God wants me to do.

If you are faced with a possible fight, I encourage you to humbly and prayerfully ask these two questions. If the answer to both clearly is no, then you need to find a way to avoid the fight. I'm not suggesting that you become a coward or run from something that needs attention. You just need to recognize that this particular situation is not as important as others.

I have often chosen not to respond to unfounded criticism because whenever you speak about something, you're acknowledging that it has some importance.

In life, you will only have enough time, resources, and energy to fight the battles that threaten your purpose.

I don't fight battles of name calling, theology, or opinions about me. None of these things will affect my destiny, so I don't want to expend energy responding to them. I also never let other people define me.

In life you have to know what deserves your energy and what does not. In summary:

The only battles deserving of your time
and energy are the ones that threaten your
destiny or take your spoils of victory.

Always remember that an enemy will make you focus. During times of plenty and peace, we relax. An enemy arising will cause you to focus on taking good things and making them great.

The enemy of "lack" caused me to restructure our entire ministry, forced us to become a well-oiled machine, and challenged us to become a good steward of the resources we had. In your job, your marriage or other relationships, and in all areas of life, sometimes God will use an enemy to force you to pay attention to details that you would normally let slip...and as a result harm comes your way.

I have even seen in my life where God lets an enemy reveal something ugly to stop something awful.

LEARNING TO STAND

Sometimes you gain victory by simply outlasting your enemy, by mustering up more perseverance than your enemy. Sometimes you just have to find the courage, strength, stamina, and faith to endure so that at the end of the game, when your enemy says, "I've had it! I give up," you're the one still standing.

In my crisis I wanted to say, "To heck with it! I didn't ask for this. I don't need this." I wanted to run, but I didn't. Some of this was my Possum Kingdom stubbornness. Most of it was grace. In all of it God deserves the glory.

Sometimes you've done everything you know to do, prayed all you know to pray, bound all you know to bind, loosed everything you know to loose, and cast out everything you know to cast out. What's left to do? You stand. You outlast your enemy, because in most cases—just like Goliath, who didn't expect David to continue running toward him when everyone else was running away—your enemy has underestimated your ability to stay on your feet in the day of trouble.

The Bible refers to us—the righteous—as being like palm trees (Psalm 92:12). I've lived most of my life in South Carolina, and whenever a torrential downpour or a major storm hits the coast, the meteorologists usually have a reporter on the beach, wearing a slicker, being beaten by the rain and wind, giving a firsthand account of the storm's severity as a warning of the potential danger. But what I'm usually paying attention to are the trees in the background. I'm always amazed that the trees that stand, despite being bent horizontal by the wind, are the palms. Palm trees bend but don't break.

That's a great picture of how we "righteous trees" are to stand when facing an enemy's onslaught. We may bend, but we don't break.

We stand.

ENEMY FOOTSTOOLS

God's intent is to make all your enemies your footstools. God will bring enemies into your life to elevate you to levels that, without them, you could never have reached.

There's no greater example of this principle than the Cross. Why? Because it was the Enemy coming against Jesus that ultimately led to the spread of the gospel. What was just one Person dying on a cross over two thousand years ago, thanks to an enemy, is now a worldwide movement of billions of people.

Could it be that the enemy coming against you is being used by God to multiply you?

Always remember...

The bigger the enemy,
the bigger the footstool.

A footstool is not just a spot to put your feet up; it is a practical piece of furniture that allows you to grasp something higher. Without a stool, there's a level you can't reach.

My maternal grandma was a pro at using stools, because she was a very short woman. She came from a farm family with a huge garden that yielded a bountiful crop, so Grandma spent much of her summer canning vegetables that the family ate the rest of the year.

At her house tons of Mason jars were stacked high on shelves. And my grandmother had a collection of wooden stools—several different heights—that she used to get the jars down that she needed. Without those stools, the family might not have had much to eat! The higher Grandma needed to reach, the higher the stool.

That illustrates how God will use an enemy footstool to lift you to the next level of His purpose for you.

ALWAYS BE A LEARNER

All of us can ultimately learn life's lessons only two ways: we can learn through an experience or learn through what someone who's wise tells us. That's why having wise people—mentors—speaking to us is so valuable. Learning from someone else's experiences, both good and bad, is so much easier than taking the knocks yourself.

You can't control everything that happens to you, but you do control your perspective and how you respond to situations. Most of the people I've met who can learn only by experience are hardheaded. At many points in their lives, God sent individuals with direction, insight, and a word from experience, but they wouldn't listen.

I have to admit that most of the pain I've experienced has come through situations when I heard someone, somewhere, at some point come before what happened and say, "Look out!"

I believe we've all ignored some red flags. The key as we move ahead is to have a pliable spirit and be teachable. Don't be rebellious, but be coachable and willing to learn from anyone.

I learn from a lot of different people in my life. Some are close friends, some are distant acquaintances, and some are consultants. Some are on staff and report to me; some are mentors to whom I look up to and allow a place in my life to learn from their voices and experiences.

Some of the greatest things in life I needed to learn were taught to me by Hope and our children. In fact, there have been times when my kids have said things so profound that I had to step back and say, "That's absolutely right! I was wrong about that!"

A teachable spirit and a humbleness to admit your ignorance or your mistake will save you a lot of pain. However, if you're a person who knows it all, then you've got a lot of heavy-hearted experiences coming your way. God can correct mistakes and turn things around. But why live your life in recovery mode?

YOU DON'T HAVE TO
ANSWER CRITICS

I believe there's a level of wisdom and maturity that finally comes to believers who realize they don't have to condemn or even answer the tongues that are speaking against them. Remember:

> **Whatever voices you recognize, you've decided to give them credibility and allowed them an entry point into your life.**

If you truly want to answer and silence critics, stay focused on your purpose and goals and achieve a level of success and breakthrough you've not experienced before. I've found that most of the thousands of leaders I have had the privilege of knowing, talking to, and leading over the last three decades understand this principle: nothing frustrates your critics more than success. So don't waste time—your most precious commodity—arguing with your critics.

Who argues with an enemy on a battlefield? You simply go full speed ahead with your assignment and fight to win. You succeed. You conquer. You do what God has called you to do, and God will take your success and condemn the tongue that has been lying against you.

CONTROL YOUR ENVIRONMENT

My experience a few years ago on a fishing trip illustrates well a powerful principle I refer to as the law of environment.

This "law" means that everything has to stay connected to its source to survive. If you take the plant from the ground, it withers. Take the fish from the ocean, it dies. And that brings me to my fishing story.

On that particular outing with three of my friends, we caught a shark. We got all excited, thinking we had just done the unthinkable—catching a predator that's known to be twenty feet long and weigh over one thousand pounds.

As we pulled the fish up onto the pier, I couldn't wait to see how big he actually was. After all, this intimidating fish strikes fear into most hearts. But after we finally got the shark onto dry land, I thought, *That's it?*

Outside his environment, that shark was puny. He didn't live up to my expectation of being twenty feet long and having a mouth the size of a doorway. On the pier, he didn't even scare us, though in the water he would have brought chill bumps.

What happens when you take a fish like that out of water? It dies. Its intimidation no longer affects you, and your fears wash away.

This shows clearly how the law of environment operates—a particular setting will lead to certain results. And here's where I'm going with this: If you bring the Enemy into *your* environment, he won't be able to operate in it. He can't come over into your worship; he needs you in a worldly, carnal environment. If you would step back into the presence of God, you'd see that you're strong in Him, you're built up in your faith and passion, and all things are possible. There you magnify Him. He gets bigger and bigger, and all your problems get smaller and smaller.

God is our life source. If we are removed from God, we begin the process of dying because we've been removed from our source. Understanding this principle is a powerful weapon in overcoming your enemy.

Remember the shark—we took him out of his environment and put him into ours, and suddenly he didn't look so terrifying anymore. Our fears and worries quickly shrank.

When you can, fight the battle on your turf. It's like the home-field advantage in sports, only much better!

PROPER EXPOSURE

When God contacted Abraham about the plan for his life, He told Abraham to drop everything and go. Genesis 12 records the Lord's command and promise to Abraham:

> Get out of your country, from your family and from your father's house, to a land that I will show you. I will make you a great nation; I will bless you and make your name great; and you shall be a blessing. (Genesis 12:1–2)

If you think that was easy for Abraham, think again. He was a wealthy man living the good life.

Notice that before God told Abraham what He was going to give him, He told him what he had to leave behind. God rarely shows you *there* until you leave *here*. And if you are trying to grab hold of two side-by-side projects at the same time, you're going to be frustrated. I've been living long enough to know that God does not let you grasp the next thing until you have released the current thing.

Most people want to walk into blessing without giving up anything. God took a moment to say to Abraham, "Before we even begin to talk about what I can do with you, you've got to get out of your country, your comfort zone, your familiarity, your safe life."

God was trying to tell Abraham that the key ingredient to his greatness was to leave what was limiting him in order to become exposed to things he had never seen before. He created a mental picture of how plentiful his future would be, but God had to get Abraham out of his familiar setting to give him this new picture. This is where an essential ingredient in fighting to win is revealed: *exposure.*

Remember my shrimp-in-the-soup incident at the country club dinner? Because I had humble beginnings, to get me to move forward in my destiny as a leader, God had to expose me to life on another level. Little did I know that my embarrassing dinner experience had nothing to do with soup. It did have everything to do with exposing me to a life I was not acquainted with so that I could understand the experiences of a broader range of people and thereby minister to them more effectively.

The same is true for all of us:

**In your progress toward God's purpose for you,
anything you hang on to that
God wants you to drop is an enemy.**

Why was it that Elisha, when called by Elijah to prophetic ministry, burned his plows (1 Kings 19:19–21)? Because he wasn't going to make room for anything to be a tempting crutch for him in his future—the day things got tough.

Your potential and your level of revelation will always be limited in life by your exposure.

It wasn't until I was playing drums in a college music group and we began traveling to various churches much larger than I had ever seen that I realized that normal churches had indoor bathrooms! I was amazed that these big churches even had a children's church. I remember thinking, *What is children's church?* Our children's church was my head laid up in my mama's lap in the third row while I slept through the message!

We want to step out of solid ground onto solid ground, but God doesn't do that. God makes you step out of something that's on a stable foundation and then makes you walk out the next season of your life on words—His promises.

THE BATTLE IS THE LORD'S

Warning! I'm going to make a powerful statement here:

**When you're pursuing your purpose, it would be
in your enemy's best interest not to fight you. But it
would be in God's best interest to have him fight.**

When enemies come against your purpose, they aren't coming against you; they're coming against God.

Proverbs says, "There are many plans in a man's heart, nevertheless the LORD's counsel—that will stand" (19:21). God's purpose always prevails, so the enemies are not standing in your way; they're standing in God's way. These are the battles in life when you get to sit back and watch "Daddy" handle your business.

How wonderful it is, when you find yourself in those difficult times, that you don't have to open your mouth or berate your enemy! God will cause your enemy to flee before your very eyes.

I had enemies that wanted to destroy my purpose, my mission, my assignment in life. This was no small thing. These people wanted a For Sale sign on the property of our ministry. I could not possibly fight all the battles. They had to be God's fight.

I had people telling me that I needed to mount my own defense in various ways, but in my heart I knew that wasn't the route to take. The battle was the Lord's. I was going to have to wait patiently and let God bring the victory. I knew He would deliver me, because my enemies were standing in the way of my purpose. When others stand in the way of your purpose, they're not picking a fight with you but with your God.

God promised Moses from a burning bush that He was going to take His people and bring them to a land flowing with milk and honey. Pharaoh stood in the way. So whose responsibility was it to take care of Pharaoh? Not Moses's or the Hebrews. No, it was God's responsibility, because Pharaoh was directly confronting their purpose.

Later they faced the Red Sea, which stood in the way. The sea had become the enemy of Israel's purpose. The horses of Egypt's army were drawing near behind them. The sea was in front of them. It was not their responsibility to swim. It was God's responsibility to remove the enemy.

No matter what stands in the way, as Scripture says, "Do not be afraid nor dismayed because of this great multitude, for the battle is not yours, but God's" (2 Chronicles 20:15).

WATCH WHAT YOU MAGNIFY

Try a quick exercise with me. Take a dime. Hold the dime between your index finger and thumb. Now, stretch your arm out as far as you can. You can still see everything in the room, right?

Okay, now slowly pull the dime in, closing your left eye, pulling it in closer and closer to the right eye. Pull the dime all the way up to your face until it's right up against the open eye. I bet you can't see anything other than the dime, right?

That's how the Enemy sometimes works. He gets you focused on things that ain't worth a dime.

Sometimes, before you go into battle, you have to get above your circumstances and reexamine how big your enemy really is.

David urged everyone, "Magnify the LORD with me" (Psalm 34:3). However, when an enemy of any kind threatens us, we shift our focus off Him and on to the enemy, and it's like taking a magnifying glass to an anthill. Through that lens, the ants look significantly larger and more terrifying than they really are.

That's why the Bible's instruction to magnify God is so powerful. God is not on an ego trip. He wants us to magnify Him because He knows that, if we do, we'll be able to defeat any enemy that comes against us and use that enemy as a stepstool for promotion to the next level in life.

Here's a way to remember this:

To get out from underneath the threat of an enemy, change what you're magnifying.

At the time of the Exodus, most of the spies who returned from Canaan magnified the enemy and described themselves through their *condition*. They were physically smaller and weaker than the inhabitants of the land, so they felt reduced to comparing themselves to grasshoppers (Numbers 13:32–33). But Joshua and Caleb saw the enemy through their *position* as the soldiers of almighty God. So they knew that they would defeat the enemy.

Do you know how big your God is? The Bible says God uses the earth as a footstool (Isaiah 66:1). He takes the whole earth and uses it as an ottoman! You serve a God *that* big, and you're worried about your upcoming job review and your car payment?

He knows the number of hairs on your entire head (Luke 12:7), yet how much time do you spend stressing over, worrying about, and looking at your problem? That's His job. You're supposed to set your eyes on Jesus, the author and finisher of your faith (Hebrews 12:2).

Here's the problem with a problem: If you keep looking at an enemy, it fills your field of vision—before long it seems that the enemy is all you can see. That's why the Bible instructs us to magnify the Lord at all times. If He fills our vision, then we are seeing what is true and ultimately real—a God with whom all things are possible.

WHO ARE YOU FOLLOWING?

When I go on vacation and I decide to hire a guide for an outing, I've committed to following someone who will take me to a place where I want to go but don't know how to get there by myself. I expect the guide to be familiar with the territory through which he is taking me. I expect him to know the path, the dangers, the people, the environment, and the cost. Frankly, I expect him to know everything important about our trip. I expect him to get me to my destination capable of enjoying it and performing whatever I'm supposed to do there.

I certainly don't want a guide who doesn't know where he is going himself. Jesus called that the blind leading the blind, saying both will end up in a ditch (Luke 6:39).

In our battle against any enemy, we hold a distinct advantage. We not only have God on our side, but we also have God on our inside—in the person of the Holy Spirit.

The apostle Paul wrote: "What man knows the things of a man except the spirit of the man which is in him? Even so no one knows the things of God except the Spirit of God. Now we have received, not the spirit of the world, but the Spirit who is from God, that we might know the things that have been freely given to us by God" (1 Corinthians 2:11–12).

The Holy Spirit knows what the Father knows, and when the Holy Spirit comes to live inside us, then He becomes our guide. I've heard so many theologians, ministers, and others try to overspiritualize this, but I think this simple explanation is accurate:

**The Holy Spirit living inside you will guide you into
the things God has for you in your life.**

The Holy Spirit has the full scouting report on you. He has gotten the information from the Father concerning your purpose and all God has predestined for your life. He's counted the cost and knows the environment, the people you'll encounter on the way, the struggles, and the conclusion of the journey.

Writing on this topic, the apostle Paul had more to add:

> Eye has not seen, nor ear heard,
> Nor have entered into the heart of man
> The things which God has prepared for those who love Him.
>   (1 Corinthians 2:9; also see Isaiah 64:4)

The consummate Guide, the Holy Spirit, reveals to me daily the life, the ways, and the intent of God for me so I can reach the ultimate end that He has planned for me.

The Spirit will guide you through every battle with every enemy and in time help you understand the meaning of it all.

Here's what I'm talking about...

At 5:00 a.m. one morning in 2000, I discovered my wife, Hope, nearly unconscious, lying in a pool of blood on our bedroom floor. She had collapsed on the way to the bathroom.

I rushed her to the hospital and learned that she had been bleeding internally and had lost much of her body's blood. The doctors told me there was a possibility she wouldn't make it. When they discovered she was hemorrhaging in her intestines, they operated and saved her life.

We thanked God for sparing her, but when she was allowed to come home, she faced a long recovery process. She needed me.

I looked at all the speaking engagements on my calendar for the next six months and canceled them all—except one. Something internally (the Guide) impressed on me that I should keep this date. Honestly, it appeared to be the most unattractive event of them all. Left to my own wisdom, it would have been the first one to cancel.

It was a very unusual commitment. I had agreed to go to a widow's home in northeast Georgia and spend an entire day talking to three couples about planting a church. I would not be speaking in a large church—in quick, then gone after the last morning service. No, this was three couples plus the widow. A whole day's investment.

I would have loved to get out of this commitment, and with my wife recovering from major surgery, I had a good reason to cancel. But on the inside, I knew by the Holy Spirit that I needed to go. Why? I hadn't a clue. But I had a strong enough sense that, if I didn't go, I would be pulling a Jonah and directly disobeying God.

Against my own will, I kept the date. And when the day came, so that Hope wouldn't have to be alone, I took her with me. Since the meeting was at a house, she could rest in an adjoining room while I visited with the others.

When I arrived, I met the widow who had invited me to her home, along with three couples—as well as a man who was by himself. I'd never met this guy before, and he basically kept to himself the entire time. He was not talkative, and he and I hardly conversed.

Not much happened that day, except it was draining for both Hope and me and appeared to have consumed valuable time.

A few weeks later I got a call from the quiet guy who had been at the widow's house. He informed me that he was editor-in-chief of a major Christian magazine. In 1999 we had begun the multicultural emphasis in our Greenville church. The editor had heard about this and decided he wanted to do an article titled "Breakthrough in the Bible Belt." A whole team came to Greenville and did a major feature article: story, pictures, interview—the whole deal. Immediately our story had national exposure.

Because of this publicity, not long afterward the president of one of the largest media corporations in America came to visit me and said, "I want to put you on secular TV. I think you're one of the few pastors who can relate to not just a Christian audience."

This sounded good, but I wondered what the catch was.

"I can do everything," he said. "I can help buy the time, get you special deals—we're a large media buyer. But you will have to get all the equipment for making your program."

I thanked the man, but when he left, I knew there was no way, no possibility whatsoever, that our ministry could afford hundreds of thousands of dollars' worth of video equipment.

Next, another minister who had read the magazine article called. It so happened that he had a large TV ministry. He wanted me to come on his program and talk about what was happening at our church. I went and learned quite a bit about TV ministry. But I still had no money for equipment.

After I got back home, the pastor with the large TV ministry called and said, "By the way, I felt like I needed to call and tell you this: Don't ever buy any of that media equipment. Always put it on lease so you can upgrade every two or three years. Don't ever pay all that cash for it."

That was an "aha" moment—"Thank You, Holy Spirit!" All of a sudden what would have cost us hundreds of thousands of dollars was now available for rent for $2,600 a month. Still not chump change, for sure, but we could afford that.

We started televising some of our services, and in a matter of months, we went from one thousand members to thousands of members. And now, some years later, our TV ministry reaches 120 nations, and we have fifteen hundred churches all over the world in our ministerial fellowship network. There are also satellite church campuses in other states.

This all started with a meeting I wanted to cancel at a widow's house in northeast Georgia—a meeting about which my Guide said, "No, you need to go there."

When we have Friends like that, our enemy doesn't stand a chance.

PART 8

THE SPOILS
OF VICTORY

In my twenty years of ministry, I have faced many enemies. Many I initially faced with great confusion and frustration, because they seemed to appear with no rhyme or reason, a series of random difficult events to endure. But when the events I've described in this book fell upon my life and I found myself faced with real trouble on every side—with the future of the church, my family, and my own emotional and physical health hanging in the balance—God led me on the study of enemies that I have now taken you on. This study was a journey that helped me achieve a proper perspective—God's perspective—as I learned that each enemy had a particular purpose, each one raised me to a new level to open a door that had previously been shut, and all of them had been working on my behalf for God to accomplish His purpose.

I cannot tell you how much this biblical journey put me at rest and at peace, not only with my God but also with the steps He had ordered for my life. I have been able to revel in the victory that has come.

For you, too, the time of victory over an enemy will come. You may not know the exact moment of victory in your battle, because defeating an enemy is often a process. But there will come a day when you know it's time to break out the party hats and "get down." The battle is over!

I've told a lot about the struggle I went through that provoked the writing of this book. Now I want to share the triumph. Good things resulted in every aspect of my life—in my family, in the ministry, in me.

I cannot pinpoint an exact moment when I knew a bright new day of my future had dawned, but there's one incident that certainly illustrates how the "promotion" ceremony was underway.

NEW GENERATION

As I've said before, one of the reasons I had a necessity for an enemy is that I had gotten stuck on autopilot at our church.

We had been greatly blessed, but what had worked for me for many years was fizzling out. For most of my twenty years in ministry, I had pastored the same group of people. That's a good thing, of course, but God wanted to shake things up. The church was at a fork in the road: we were doing a ton of ministry but also were not attracting many younger people, especially into the leadership ranks.

I decided to bring this to a head and called a meeting of the whole church. I sat down on a stool and said, "Everybody my age and up, raise your hand." At that time I was about forty, and about half the people there were as old as or older than I and responded by raising their hands. "I'm going to make it my business as your pastor," I said, "to go hard after your children." That pleased the more mature group I had singled out, and they gave me a standing ovation.

"Now, everybody my age and down, raise your hand," I went on. This time, again, about half the people there responded. "All right, I'm going to place new levels of demand on you younger people. Statistics show me that you come to church, but your mama and daddy pay the bills—and they do most of the volunteer work too. So if I'm going to restructure the church for your generation, you must step up to new levels of responsibility!"

Again, I had hit a good nerve and got another standing ovation. Everybody stood up this time!

So that's what we started to do—change our church so we could reach younger people. And before long I came to a profound conclusion about life:

Every vision is celebrated until it's implemented!

Most churches have one generation that takes that church to greatness, but then because they are all quite happy with where they have "arrived," they find it hard to make the changes that will attract and hold their children—the next generation. The organization begins to die a slow death. It's a sad thing to watch.

Some folks from the maturing generation—the ones who had given me loud applause—became uncomfortable with all the changes that began to happen and, sadly, started leaving the church. But we succeeded in allowing our church to (as I call it) "jump the curve."

So now I can report that, in our church, the founding generation is beginning to phase out, and we are transitioning to minister to the Internet, high-tech generation at a rapid pace. Our church has never grown like this before!

Without the enemies that came against me in the battle over the single moms' program, all these changes in me and the church staff and in the vision for the church would never have happened—guaranteed. You've heard before that the enemy of great is good. I had it good! But God wanted to take the ministry to a place of *great* impact.

It's that seed principle again: in significant ways we had to fall into the plowed ground and die so a new thing could sprout and grow. A difficult, beautiful process.

When the generation we had ministered to for so long began to grow unsatisfied with the church, I saw such enemies as accusation, betrayal, apathy, and discouragement raise their heads. However, the victory over each enemy led to exponential, explosive growth that opened doors to other spheres of influence into which our ministry would otherwise never have had access.

The young adult generation was showing up. With a new team of leaders possessing a fierce loyalty to the vision, we began implementing one hundred satellite Internet churches across the United States, saw the opening of several businesses that would feed revenue streams into the church to support further ministry, and witnessed the voice of our church televised into 120 nations.

All these opportunities didn't exist until an enemy came to announce that

God was about to enlarge our territory and expand our tent. As difficult as the battles were, and as fierce as the enemies fought, I wouldn't trade today's harvest for anything, because God's prize is always worth the pain of the process.

And along the way I've discovered many other truths about what happens after a victory.

PROPERTY LINES

I live in a subdivision. I have never awakened to find my neighbor raking my leaves, and he's never come home to me cutting his grass. Why? Because there's a property line between our houses. He's responsible for what's within his borders, and I'm responsible for what's inside my borders.

There's a lesson for us here.

You have to properly define what's in your care and what's not. Give proper oversight to what is yours, and release to God what you can't control.

By allowing ministry and its troubles to dominate so much of my life, I had let my emotional health be affected. After being misused, accused, and betrayed, I waited for certain people to come and apologize or come and fix me and restore me. Then I remembered the property line around my emotional health. These were leaves I had to rake, grass I had to cut.

It was at that moment that I made a decision to never put my emotional health in the hands of anyone else. I realized that in every situation, even where I feel a great injustice has been done or my trust has been violated, it's my responsibility to guard my emotional health; it's not someone else's responsibility to come and apologize and heal me.

You're going to have to reach the same kind of "aha" moment about your own responsibilities, especially if your battle occurred in the area of your gifting.

The gifts God gave you—the ones you use to bring Him glory—do not strengthen you. In fact, using them to serve others depletes you. Through my serious encounters with enemies, I learned this lesson the hard way:

There's a big, critical difference
between your gifting and you.

Ron's gift is not Ron.

Jesus never became close friends with people who followed Him only because of His gift, and that's a powerful and critical distinction to recognize. Your gift is not you. Furthermore, although your gift is God-given and will serve you well when enemies rise up against you, your gift drains you. This is another reason you need to be intentional about cultivating friendships with people who don't really need your gift. True friends just like being with you and thus don't constantly pull on your gift and deplete you.

A lot of people can have access to Ron's gift, but only a few people can have Ron. Those people are Ron's family. This I learned because of the enemies that came against my life. I learned the power of setting boundaries.

There's a reason the ocean can come only so far. The ocean is enjoyable as long as its boundaries, the shoreline, are properly defined. When it goes beyond its boundaries, destruction sets in.

The enemies I faced made me ask these questions: *How far will I let ministry come into my house? How far can other people's drama come into my home? To what extent am I willing to sacrifice my family to help others?*

I realized I had to make some changes. For example, no more seventy-hour workweeks. In the past, the old Ron never met a ministry opportunity he didn't like. I was always on call. Virtually anything had the potential to interrupt our family life.

Like the time we had a big weekend planned to take the kids to the state zoo. But then I got a call and was invited to speak at a major conference—it was the biggest opportunity to strut my stuff that I'd ever had. So guess what happened to the zoo trip plans? Postponed indefinitely.

I've had to repent for bad choices like that. I was humbled during my battles with enemies.

I have learned how to say no. I figured out how to cut off the lights, shut the door, and leave the office at the office. I learned how not to answer a ringing or buzzing phone—no matter what the need on the other end of the line. I learned how to place a reasonable separation between me and what I do.

What about your property lines? Though these may be tough decisions for you, there are probably some boundaries you need to reassess in your life.

THE AFTERMATH OF AN ENEMY

I previously shared that a fight makes you focus. That focus had better continue even after the battle.

We all need times to put down our swords and let our hair down, so to speak. But after a battle you still need to maintain a sense of guardedness in your life. You're not nearly as vulnerable in a fight as you are when you relax.

Noah, although mocked daily by his neighbors, was steadfast, focused, and determined to complete the mission of preparing for the Flood. He spent decades building the ark, then set sail with every animal on the planet (including some ferocious and dangerous ones!) and his family. And he got it done.

But when the floodwaters receded and the ark came to rest, what did Noah do? He went out and got drunk. He got too comfortable, and it led to an embarrassment that such a great patriarch should never have gone through. The Bible tells us that his sons looked upon his nakedness, which was a great shame in those days (Genesis 9:20–27).

And of course Noah wasn't the only one.

When kings were normally at war, King David was at home, enjoying the fruits of his earlier victories in solidifying the nation's might. It was a time for kings to be at a battle, yet he wasn't in his rightful place. So he ended up being in places where he shouldn't have been, planning what he shouldn't have been planning, doing what he shouldn't have been doing (2 Samuel 11).

The point I'm trying to make is that you can be most vulnerable in the best times of your life—your times of savoring your victory. Too many times, I see wonderful people allow the aftermath of a battle to carry them into a drunken, lustful, or other inappropriate state and get caught unaware by an enemy they'd forgotten about. You may forget about your enemy, but your enemy hasn't forgotten about you.

A day that should be your greatest day of celebration can produce your biggest season of shame if you allow yourself to drop your guard and become vulnerable.

What about you? How will you respond after victory?

I will tell you that these are the best of times, but if you are not on guard, you will find yourself right back in another battle.

Remember: The Enemy doesn't go on vacation. He's looking for someone to eat. You look kind of fat and tasty now!

Let's gain some more insight from the story of the triumphant prophet Elijah (1 Kings 18–19).

Elijah had just taken on all the prophets of Baal, took them to the river, and executed them. But then Queen Jezebel threatened to take him out, and he fell apart. What was going on?

Think about it. This guy just had, arguably, one of his best days ever. He called down fire from heaven. He killed hundreds of prophets, destroyed and cut up a bull, even outran a chariot on the way home. You have to be pretty adrenalin-infused from a victory to be able to outrun a chariot! But he got one threat from an enemy, and he had to run to his mommy!

I don't know all the reasons Elijah acted the way he did, but his example points to the fact that the aftermath of a victory is a vulnerable time. If it can happen to an all-pro spiritual warrior like Elijah, it can happen to you and me.

A battle takes a lot out of you. And if your fight has been in an external arena, like Elijah's, you will need some downtime and an opportunity to rest and experience healing.

ENVIRONMENTAL CHANGE

It's hard to get healed in familiar places.

Sometimes, for God to do a real work of change in your life, He has to remove you from a familiar environment and move you into a safe place.

Often when I'm emotionally drained or I've reached a place of extreme discouragement, I have to remove myself from my normal environment and go to a place where I'm not recognized by my titles, by my gifts, or by my role in life. God has to move me to a place where I'm just Ron, and God is God, and I can be changed without the fear of other people's opinions while I'm being healed.

I think the experience of Naaman, which I've already discussed, gives some insight on how to effectively heal in this way after a major battle. This successful military leader had to go from Syria to Israel to find help. This illustrates that it is difficult to receive rest and healing in your daily environment. Usually you will have to pull away from the routine and your normal life setting to receive restoration. As Psalm 23:2–3 says, you may need to be led by still waters to be restored.

In Bible times, they didn't have good mirrors, so they'd use still waters to get a reflection of how they looked. This is why the language of the psalmist is so compelling. He takes you to a place—still waters—where you can get a reflection of who you really are without the disturbances of the rocks that life will throw at you to distort you.

God has to get you to a safe place where He can heal you and help you regain your strength.

**It's rare to receive healing in the environment
you work and live in every day.**

You get tired when your mind gets tired. You get tired when you're emotionally drained. Never make big decisions when you're tired, because your perceptions are off and you're usually not seeing your circumstances correctly.

Weariness turns molehills into mountains.

Don't get a divorce, leave a job, or make some other significant decision when you're tired. Tired is a feeling, and feelings change. When you're recovering from a major battle, you have to be mature enough to recognize and remember that the things you see when you're that tired are always magnified.

Those times of fatigue are when you need to allow God to take you to safe places and allow safe voices to speak to you.

You may not be able to go away by leaving town, but in some way, for at least a short period of time—even a few hours—you need to find a way to change your environment so the Holy Spirit can help you see reality and adjust your perspective. And bring needed rest and healing.

RECALIBRATION

The Bible makes it clear that in this world we will have trials and tribulations (John 16:33). After a great battle with an enemy, you'll often have to recalibrate from a new position where the battle has left you.

I'm not good with directions, as Hope will attest.

Not long ago, when traveling somewhere we had never been before, I asked the on-board navigation system for help while I drove. But I got so caught up in the music we were listening to and the alone time I was enjoying with my wife that I tuned out the voice of the navigation system. As a result I missed a series of turns, and suddenly we were lost and had to pull over.

How did I recover? Thankfully the navigation system was still on, even though I had missed a turn. It was still ready to communicate with me if I would listen. As Hope and I sat on the side of the road, we watched the digital screen, where a bar was traveling from left to right. The word under the bar? "Recalibrating."

Like magic, the system determined the new location, as off track as I was, and began giving me new instructions to get to our destination. Based on my new position, it had recalibrated the road map for me so that I could still arrive at my intended end.

God does the same kind of thing for us. We miss a couple of turns in life. Maybe we weren't paying attention when God was speaking. Maybe we intentionally chose another voice over His.

And so sometimes, especially after a hard-fought battle, we end up at places we never expected or wanted to be. I've learned that God is even in that wrong turn and miscalculation, because the lessons learned along the way will help you in an even more powerful way the next time you face a new enemy and a new battle.

The good news is:

Just because an opportunity was missed does not mean it is lost forever.

God's system of recalibration is explained so well in Romans 8:28: "All things work together for good to those who love God, to those who are the called according to His purpose." What peace and rest that scripture brings me, to know that God has already made provision for His purpose to prevail, even though I might make a bad decision or two along the way!

And there's another verse that, if anything, brings me even greater comfort: "In Him also we have obtained an inheritance, being predestined according to the purpose of Him who works *all things* according to the counsel of His will" (Ephesians 1:11, emphasis added). Catch that? In the end, absolutely "all things," even our greatest struggles, will conform to God's magnificent will.

So if you're sitting there, thinking, *Man, my life is a mess,* I have something to say to you: No matter what mistake you made, your God has the ability to massage your mistakes back into His perfect plan. God can always recalibrate your life. No matter where you are on earth, a man-made satellite never loses you. And your God is better than any man-made satellite. He knows you because He made you, He knows right where you are because He went there with you, and He knows the way out because He made it before you ever went in.

Opportunities come in cycles, and you just have to wait for the next one to come along and for the door to reopen.

God will take care of us while we're recalibrating. He'll create special moments when restoration and healing will come. He'll open the faucet and relieve the pressure by giving us times when emotions that were damaged can be healed and strength that was lost can be restored.

God's always there to guide us. He recalculates our journey for us depending on where we are now.

WHAT'S NEXT?

What do you do after a tough battle when, even if you "won," you now feel strangely empty and the next season of your life is unclear?

A dilemma that compounds the problem is that life usually does not stop long enough for anyone to recuperate. Most people do not get the luxury of stopping life from moving and having time to deal with the latest turn in life.

Back to the prophet Elijah: His whole ministry had been about fighting for Israel's heart, but now the battle was finally over, and he wanted to die. The great prophet was stuck right in the middle of transition and was having trouble seeing himself in a new form.

Elijah was at the pinnacle of his life, and that's usually when people hit depression. They've reached the pay scale they always dreamed of achieving, the kids are finally off to college, or they've obtained some other major milestone.

Then something profound took place. God fed Elijah twice, and I believe each feeding had an important meaning (1 Kings 19:5–8). The angel came to feed Elijah the first time to put him to sleep. He came the second time to give Elijah new vision.

When you've been through a tough battle, as Elijah had, there is a time when God feeds you what you need to recover. This season may vary with different people. Some people recuperate fast; others, slowly. Regardless, there are blessings, times in His presence, that are refreshing, to help heal wounds from yesterday's battles and turn your scabs into scars.

Do you know the difference between a scab and a scar? A scab is a place where you've been wounded, and if you hit it, it will continue to bleed. A scar is where a wound once was, and you can tell that something happened, but the scar is proof that the wound has been healed. Finally, once it's a scar, you don't bleed anymore.

Once the first meal has been served to heal you, hold on! There's another meal coming that is visionary—it opens your eyes to let you know there's more going for you than going against you.

The first meal heals your past; the second sets your future.

When you're down, your perception's off. Elijah wanted to die, but God said, "I've got seven thousand faithful ones waiting for you! You're so down that you can't see." Elijah wasn't in his worst day; he was in his best. He had to have one meal to recover, then another for his future, to allow him to hope again.

The key takeaway here for your life is:

Just because your life is transitioning doesn't mean it's ending.

Give God, and yourself, the opportunity to regroup as one season ends and another begins.

AN ATMOSPHERE
FOR HEALING

In the aftermath of a battle, there still may be brokenness that needs healing. Many people have tried over and over again to quit habits, break addictions, or conceal some things that no one knows anything about, only for those things to continue operating in their lives and eventually cause them to give up hope in anything ever changing.

Jesus always had a way of creating an atmosphere where weakness could be revealed, but we have developed in families, in friendships, and especially in churches today an atmosphere where weaknesses are hidden. This pressure to be okay and not have our problems show isolates us further from the people and places we should be able to go to for healing of our internal struggles. The places where we need to be to get healing become the very places in which we have to conceal our problems.

Jesus went up to the man with the withered hand and said, "Stretch out your hand" (Mark 3:5). Notice that Jesus never said which hand the man was to stretch out. If this guy came into most churches today, he would reach out his good hand, expecting that that's what Jesus would want him to do. Few people in the church atmosphere would feel that they could stretch out the hand that does not work correctly.

That's not how Jesus approached the problems we all have.

**Jesus created an atmosphere where
weaknesses could be healed.**

I long to see church, friendships, and relationships be places where weaknesses can be revealed without being judged.

If you are in a place where you cannot extend your withered hand and find the healing you need, look for some other place where you can. Ask the Holy Spirit to guide you to the people who will allow you to be vulnerable. Find a place with the "Jesus atmosphere."

ON THE BANKS
OF THE RIVER

I've talked about the suffering my wife and family endured. Now I can't wait to tell you about the healing in my home.

It had to start with me.

Sometimes a Goliath has to get in your
face to bring about needed changes.

As I have already said, in the past I did not have good boundaries between my ministry and my family. Now I want to tell you what establishing boundaries did for my family.

A proper boundary promotes health on both sides of the division. In Ezekiel there's an image of a river that beautifully pictures such a boundary. On both banks of this river "grow all kinds of trees used for food; their leaves will not wither, and their fruit will not fail.... Their fruit will be for food, and their leaves for medicine" (Ezekiel 47:11–12). In other words, where there is a solid boundary, great health and healing are found. But the opposite is true as well: when the waters of life are not properly contained within banks, they flow out randomly and become a swamp.

My life had been like that—all the activity of ministry swirling out and mixing in through my home, forming a swamp. So, in the midst of all our personal devastation, with Hope struggling with depression and my health withering under the stress, we took an inventory of our personal and ministry priorities.

It was not good enough having enemies propel me to new levels just in my ministry. Even though I love the call on my life, the real love of my life (after God) is my wife and family. I began to take personal inventory of my priorities.

Without having experienced the havoc that these enemies had wreaked in my home, I would never have taken the time to reprioritize and reinvest in my family like I needed to. I made a renewed commitment after the smoke had cleared from all my battles. I know I'm not the world's greatest husband, but I committed myself to be the kind of husband who values everything my wife brings to my life—the way she runs our home, the homework time she devotes to our kids, the special touch she gives to every home-cooked meal, the way she wears my favorite perfume. I had once again found the long-lost sweet spot in life where every little thing is precious to me. Even a simple look from my wife gets a tender response, and every meal gets a heartfelt thank-you. My enemies have brought depth to the relationships in our home and caused a fabric of intimacy to be woven that never existed before.

For me personally, these were huge steps, in part because of what else was going on in my life at the time. You see, while I was making these recommitments to marriage and family, simultaneously the whole world was opening up to my ministry. Suddenly my staff wanted more time from me. An ever-growing community of pastors coming under our oversight wanted more of me. And so, while all these blessings were coming on one side, I had to learn how to say no, for the sake of things that are more important.

I know that without the battles that came with the single moms' housing program, I would not be so in love with life, my wife, and my family as I am today. I realized one day that I had reached a place personally where something big had to happen to get my attention. And it did.

I realized I was in a place where many of the little blessings and joys of life had lost their meaning. However, these battles had once again caused me to recommit myself to the simple side of life and experience great joy and satisfaction with something as simple as planting flowers with my wife or grilling hamburgers with my family. You don't realize sometimes how much life will rob you of precious moments…until an enemy arises and threatens all that you love the most.

The impact of defeating these enemies on my wife, Hope, has been nothing short of a miracle. I've watched my wife rise from the ashes of a terrible depression to become one of the most powerful women of God I have ever seen. Her faith amazes me. Her strength and courage are an inspiration. I've learned a lot about how to fight life's enemies from watching her own determination to rise above life's difficulties and move to new levels of faith and influence. Doors of opportunity have opened up to my wife that were unthinkable until a couple of years ago.

Another example. I remember seeing my son, who had to be removed from school because of anxiety, panic attacks, and OCD, now celebrating going to a regular high school. You have no idea the miracle it is, seeing the report card of a child who once was thought to be disadvantaged and who is now walking tall as one of the top students in his class.

Paul summed it up so well when he noted that once you get past the adversary, there's an amazing door opening for you (1 Corinthians 16:9). I've seen it…and walked through. You can too.

How bitter the battle, but how sweet the victory!

SO... WHAT ABOUT YOU?

f you were sitting in my church service right now, soft music would begin to play, and I would shift my focus from sharing my struggle and victory to probing into your heart about what effect life's battles have had on your home and the toll they have taken on your life.

You may have faced enemies close to you, or your enemy may have been something that happened to you. Maybe it was a decision you made that you later came to regret. Maybe you've faced enemies caused by things that were out of your control.

Whatever your situation, here's my question and my challenge: What are you going to do? How will you respond? My father once told me that life is made up of 10 percent what happens to you and 90 percent how you respond to it. How are you going to respond?

Some people see an enemy and they run. David even said in Psalm 55:6, "Oh, that I had wings like a dove! I would fly away and be at rest." If that's your instinct, let me urge you to stay put, keep fighting, and see what God will do.

I remember hearing a great personal friend and mentor, Bishop T. D. Jakes, preaching a New Year's Eve service. In services like that, it's popular preacher rhetoric to make statements such as, "Next year you'll have a new life. New marriage. New job. New bank account balance. New boss." Bishop Jakes, however, on that day, made this statement: "The fact is, when you go back to life, you'll have the same boss, same company, same bank account, and you'll be married to the same person." But, he said, life could be different in the new year if we reacted differently. The message was called "Same Old World, Brand-New You."

My battles didn't leave with the reciting of a prayer and the memorizing of a few scriptures. It was a daily process of implementing everything God had ever taught me. But the greatest weapon I had was God giving me a fresh perspective about how an enemy can be a blessing in disguise.

I wish I could tell you that reading this book will fix all of tomorrow's problems. That's not a promise I can make. I do hope this book has given you a fresh biblical perspective that enemies are indicators, announcements, clues that there's something great inside you yet to be born.

The Enemy is there, trying to ensure that your potential never manifests itself. However, the fact that he is present means there's something about your future he fears. Just having this knowledge alone is ammunition for your battle because it speaks a word to you that you have not yet lived your greatest days and that God truly does save the best for last.

If your enemies are loud and the battles are raging, continue to stand, knowing this:

Something great is about to dawn on your life.

SMALL-GROUP STUDY GUIDE

HOW TO USE THIS STUDY GUIDE

This study guide is designed for you and the members of your small group to use *after* reading the part(s) assigned to each session. The goal is for you to dive deeper, wrestle harder, and sense God's presence and affirmation through processing and praying about what you are learning.

The study guide has seven sessions. However, if your group wants to move faster or more slowly, simply adjust the reading assignments and use of questions accordingly.

1. Read the chapters.

   Each session (except number 4) covers one part of *The Necessity of an Enemy*. As you read the chapters, make notes or highlight passages in the book that speak to, challenge, or apply to you *personally*. In your reading and reflection, ask the Lord to reveal insights so that when you come to the study guide section, you will be equipped to benefit the most from the questions.

2. Pray and begin the discussion.

   At the start of each session, spend some time in prayer together. Next, one person should read the brief review aloud to remind everyone of the focus of the discussion. The leader should then invite the group to share any questions, concerns, "aha" moments, insights, or comments arising out of their personal time with the material.

3. Read the key scripture aloud.

   The key scripture is a verse or short biblical passage directly related to the theme of the part or parts being considered in that session. It's ideal for memorizing. And of course you can consult your Bible at any time to bring in other relevant Bible passages to enrich your discussion.

4. Go through the questions.

The questions are designed to focus on how each person in the group related to the main topics of the parts. Remember, the questions are there to serve the group and encourage discussion, not to elicit a particular answer. With that in mind, *don't race through the questions.* Take your time and allow the Holy Spirit to work. It is also not necessary to "go around the table" or "the circle" before you move on to the next question. The best discussions occur when people feel free to speak into the discussion. The group discussion is actually an opportunity to allow God's Spirit to minister uniquely through one believer to another in specific ways. Relax and trust God to take the discussion where He wants to take it. Remember, if God isn't in this, you are wasting your time anyway. If you don't get through all the questions for a session, no worries.

5. Note the "to remember" statements.

These are a few of the impact statements from the part or parts under discussion. They help to crystallize the focus of what you're considering. You may want to adopt some of these as mottoes for living.

6. Close each session in prayer.

Praying together is the most powerful way to make your discussion effective, meaningful, and authentic. Do not neglect it! Share your requests with others in the group. Expect God to hear and respond to your prayers. The study guide provides a prayer that you can use as is or adapt as you see fit.

Before your first session:

Please read the introductory material and part 1 of *The Necessity of an Enemy* before getting together with your group for session 1. As you do so, think about your personal experience in battling an enemy.

SESSION 1

Based on the introductory material (page 1) and part 1, "The Necessity" (page 15)

Review:

Isn't it stunning to realize that Jesus called Peter "Satan" and called Judas "Friend"? Peter, by objecting to Christ's upcoming sacrifice, was standing in the way of Jesus's mission of winning salvation for sinners. But Judas, through his betrayal of Jesus (as wicked as that was), helped Jesus accomplish that mission.

The author of *The Necessity of an Enemy*, Ron Carpenter Jr., also experienced an enemy. His enemy came in the form of an unjust lawsuit over a scam he had nothing to do with. This experience got him thinking about the nature of enemies in our lives. We all face enemies, he concluded, but if we understand them, we can use them to cooperate with the movement of God in our lives.

But why are enemies necessary? Because God has assigned a purpose to each of our lives. Satan tries to thwart that purpose by using enemies to stymie us. God, in His turn, subverts Satan's attempts so that our purpose isn't hindered but advanced.

Key scripture:

"Our light affliction, which is but for a moment, is working for us a far more exceeding and eternal weight of glory" (2 Corinthians 4:17).

Questions:

1. If you don't already know the members of your small group very well, ask:

- What is your name?
- Is there anything you want to say about your family, work, or favorite leisure activities?
- Why are you interested in reading and discussing this book?

2. *The Necessity of an Enemy* is based on a provocative idea: that the hard things we're going through can be opportunities to move ahead in

God's plan. "The right fight can be a good thing in your life," says the author. *What's your initial reaction to the idea behind this book? Are you already on board with it, or are you more skeptical? Why?*

3. The author defines an *enemy* this way: "any circumstance, any person, any deep-seated sin, any crippling character flaw—really anything the devil can dream up—that threatens the completion of God's purpose for your life." *What would you identify as the enemy (or enemies) you're facing right now? What's the battle been like for you? What harm has the enemy (or enemies) inflicted on you?*

4. Standing behind your enemy is *the* Enemy—Satan, the adversary of all whom God loves. For a moment, do what military strategists do and try to think like your enemy. *Why would Satan want the particular enemy in your life to succeed?*

5. What the devil means for harm, God turns to good. That's why the author describes the appearance of an enemy as a potential turning point: "The arrival of an enemy in your life is a sign to you that this present season you're in is finally coming to an end." *How would you describe the season of life you're in right now? What season do you believe (or at least hope) that God is going to take you into next? How can your battle help in that transition?*

6. The battleground in your life is the fulfillment of God's purpose for you. *As best you understand it right now, what is God's purpose for your life? If you're uncertain about it, who can you talk to, or what can you do, to begin getting a clearer picture of your purpose?*

7. *What questions do you hope to find answers for as you continue to read and discuss this book?*

Prayer:

> *Dear God, to be honest, it's a challenge for us to see our battles as opportunities. But we ask You to open our eyes to see our circumstances as You see them. Fill us with courage to prevail over our enemies in such a way that Your purpose is fulfilled in us— and the devil goes away grinding his teeth. By faith, we accept the adventure You're taking us on. In Jesus's name, amen.*

To remember:

- There's a Goliath, a Pharaoh, a Satan standing between you and who you are destined to become.
- An enemy arising in your life is a key indicator that the next stage of your future is about to be born.
- God has intent about every person's life, which means no one was a mistake.

For next time:

Please read part 2, "The Plan," before getting back together with your group for session 2. Be alert to signs that God intends to use your battle with your enemies to fulfill His purposes in your life.

SESSION 2

Based on part 2, "The Plan" (page 27)

Review:

It's a privilege for us to progressively discover and live out our purpose in life. But we need to know that it paints a bull's-eye on each of our backs, for Satan wants to defeat our purpose whenever he can. And this isn't just a matter of his preventing us from *doing* something; he's trying to prevent us from *being* the people God intended us to be.

So we're engaged in a long-term—indeed lifelong—battle. Our God-given potential lies within us like a seed. Satan is trying to snatch that seed away before it can take root, grow, and flower. God, meanwhile, is patiently working to preserve our purpose and make us bear fruit. And because He sees the future, He knows already that we *will* accomplish all He intends for us. Test after test, level by level, we're rising to the place He has established for us.

Key scripture:

"He who has begun a good work in you will complete it until the day of Jesus Christ" (Philippians 1:6).

Questions:

1. Ron says, "What an awesome responsibility we each have to discover our individual purpose, because it will affect not only our lives but also the lives of other people now and for generations." *Remind the group of what you think your God-given purpose is. How do you think your purpose will affect your life? How might it affect the lives of others?*

2. "Just as much as God intends for your assignment to be completed," says the author, "there is an enemy who intends for it to never take

place. That's why you can't ever give up." *Remind the group of what you see as your current enemy (or enemies). Lately, have you been tempted to give up in your battle? How can the rest of the group help you keep going?*

3. Here's a truth Satan doesn't want to accept: "Whatever identity God has established for you, that's what you are, and battling an enemy will bring that identity to light when you face and defeat that enemy." *How is battling your current enemy helping you to clarify your life purpose?*

4. Part 2 warns against getting impatient about God bringing His purpose to fruition in our lives, since God's perspective on time is very different from ours. *If you've been impatient about an improvement in your situation, describe what that's been about. What do you think it will take for you to trust—and rest—in God's timing?*

5. Speaking about the devil, the author says, "He is after the dream that has not been born, the vision that has not come to pass. He is after the you that you can be, the identity and the life you're not living out yet." This is the seed concept: your purpose lies inside you like a seed, and God and the devil are both contending over it. *Describe your "seed"— your potential—as best you understand it.*

6. Ron says, "If God has started something in your life, He already knows that it has been completed." *What do you think this means?* He goes on to say, "And He wants you to begin seeing it the same way." *How can you do that?*

7. According to part 2, a time of testing evaluates what you have learned in the previous season of your life. *What is your current battle with your enemy testing you on? Are you passing or failing, and why?*

8. *Right now, where does your confidence level stand about gaining victory over your enemy? Why?* Remember this promise from part 2: "God, in His greatness, has a way to take your right, your wrong, your good, your bad, your apathy, your ambition, your mistakes, and your successes—to take it all and make it fit the picture of your life that He crafted from the very beginning."

Prayer:

> *Lord, we're beginning to see how high the stakes really are in the battles we're facing in our lives. Don't let the devil destroy the seed You've planted in each of us! Help us to prevail over our enemies and fulfill the potential You've given us. Show us what we need to learn at each stage in our lives. Do much good through us, we ask, and we'll give You the glory. In Christ's name, amen.*

To remember:

- To God, your life is a finished picture, beautifully painted on a canvas, and He is watching parts of it unfold every day.
- Real trouble will not come in life to challenge what you're doing; it will come to test who you are.
- Every day on earth you are actually becoming what you already are!

For next time:

Please read part 3, "The Target," before getting back together with your group for session 3. Pray for God to give you His perspective on the persecution you are facing.

SESSION 3

Based on part 3, "The Target" (page 55)

Review:

The battle we're engaged in with our enemy is not fun. It's not easy. But if we look at it in the right way—from God's perspective—that will make all the difference.

Jesus told us to consider that we are blessed when we are persecuted. *Blessed.* How about that for a different way of looking at hard circumstances! But it's true: fighting the good fight against an enemy leads us into the future God has planned for us. That *is* blessing.

In the midst of persecution, we have to see with the eyes of faith. God has planted an image inside us of what He wants to do through us. We have to believe in it and, by faith, work to make it a reality. Instead of letting the Enemy distract us with the trouble that's going on around us, we have to stay focused on what God has said to us. We have to ignore the negative things said by others that would draw us away from our purpose. We have to wait in the expectancy that God will bring about what He's promised, ready to act when the opportunity comes.

And it will.

Key scripture:

"Blessed are those who are persecuted for righteousness' sake, for theirs is the kingdom of heaven" (Matthew 5:10).

Questions:

1. *What kind of persecution, if any, are you currently undergoing?*
   (Keep in mind that persecution doesn't always mean being boiled in oil. It can also mean more subtle mistreatment, such as being dissed or ignored.)

2. Commenting on Matthew 5:10, Ron says, "When you've got people misunderstanding you, lying to you, and coming against you, God says He wants you to start praising, because the fact that they're talking about you means *you are blessed*!" *What testimony can you give that this surprising statement is true?*

3. The author refers to what he calls a *faith image.* "It is an image God gives you that you can fulfill by your faith," he explains. "You can bring it to pass and make it a living reality." *What is the faith image God has given you?*

4. The devil wants you to live by *sight*—focusing on the threatening things you see all around you. God wants you to live by *faith*—trusting what He's told you. *Describe the faith/sight dilemma you find yourself in right now.*

5. *How have negative people been trying to weaken your passion for your dream? How has God been trying to fan the flame of that passion?*

6. Part 3 defines waiting in active terms. It's like sitting in ambush—you're crouched and alert, ready to spring into action whenever God gives you an opportunity to fulfill the dream He's placed in your heart. *What do you need to do to wait like that for victory against your enemy?*

7. Ron says that Satan is "being used as a pawn of God, a catapult to propel you toward your destiny." *What evidence do you see of this in your life?*

Prayer:

> *Thank You for allowing us to fight the battles we're in, Lord, for we realize they are necessary for us to achieve Your great and good purposes. But it's hard, Lord. Our suffering is vivid; the image of Your plan within us is dim. So strengthen our faith. Help us to see what You want us to see. And bring us through the season of persecution to a new season of victory and advance. Amen.*

To remember:

- Your perspective on persecution will impact your process, plans, and potential.
- The opposite of faith is sight.
- An enemy will always try to weaken your passion for your dream.
- If you are passively living life, it's going to pass you right by and your enemies will tear you to pieces.

For next time:

Please read parts 4 and 5 of *The Necessity of an Enemy* before getting back together with your group for session 4. Take note of the skirmishes and assaults carried out in the battlefield of your mind.

SESSION 4

Based on part 4, "The Enemy Within" (page 71), and part 5, "Weapons of Mass Destruction" (page 97)

Review:

Parts 4 and 5 have something in common: they're both about the spiritual fighting that goes on *inside* us—in our hearts and minds.

In part 4 Ron says, "Sometimes the toughest foe to conquer is the one living beneath your own skin." Our minds can imagine fetters that keep us in a prison that doesn't even exist. Our flesh, or sinful natures, can draw us into doing something that our spirit knows is wrong. Our natural human weakness can present openings for our enemy to do its worst. Our doubts can prevent us from trusting the leading of the Lord.

Following up, in part 5 Ron describes weapons of mass destruction our enemy can use against us. Ron says, "They're so dangerous because...they tend to be unobtrusive. They are often stealthy, silent, and disguised. Their appearance is gradual, and instead of mounting a frontal attack, they tend to snipe at you from behind over time and wear you down."

- Weapon 1: Isolation
- Weapon 2: The immature kid in you
- Weapon 3: Out-of-control feelings
- Weapon 4: False ideas about yourself
- Weapon 5: Hidden fears
- Weapon 6: Resurrection of an old thing
- Weapon 7: Ignorance
- Weapon 8: Pride
- Weapon 9: Familiarity
- Weapon 10: Bad thinking

Key scripture:

"As [a man] thinks in his heart, so is he" (Proverbs 23:7).

Questions:

1. Ron tells the story of his dog that wouldn't pass an invisible electric fence even when the dog was not wearing the specialized collar. *How is a past struggle limiting your freedom and initiative today—simply by acting upon your mind?*

2. *Can you think of a time when you blamed the devil for something you did wrong, when in fact you needed to take the blame yourself? If so, describe it. If not—without using names—describe a time when you heard someone else do this.*

3. Ron says, "One thing God despises is when someone throws away a long-term blessing to satisfy a temporary desire." *If you're willing, give an example of a time when your "flesh," or sinful nature, led you to indulge in an ungodly desire. What were the costs?*

4. In part 4 Ron explores a fascinating passage in Isaiah 10 that speaks about an ox growing so "fat," or large, that it breaks the yoke from its own neck. Ron says this means that, through steady spiritual growth, we can in time throw off the burden that our enemy has put upon us. *What spiritual practices are you engaging in to ensure long-term growth in Christ? What hope do they give you for victory over your enemies?*

5. In a military battle, one side will often concentrate its firepower on the other side's weakest point. And it's the same in spiritual warfare. The Enemy attacks your dominant weakness, whether that's pride, lust, poor self-esteem, or whatever. *What is your dominant weakness, and how have you been attacked there? What can you do to shore up your defenses in that area of your life?*

6. *Have you ever struggled with depression? If so, what advice can you give about dealing with it in a wise and godly way?*

7. Ron says that sometimes we're like Peter, who went back to his old career of fishing when Jesus died—we "keep the boat around just in case." In other words, instead of fully committing to follow Jesus, we hold on to a backup plan in case things don't work out the way we want. *Do you have a "boat"? What is your "boat"?*

8. Part 5 describes ten weapons our enemy can use against us. *Which of these weapons has done the most damage in your life, and how? Mention one or two.*

Prayer:

> *Lord, we confess that we are responsible for many of the setbacks we've experienced. Forgive us. And then strengthen our minds, spirits, and wills to resist the encroachment of the Enemy. May Your power be so evident within us that the Enemy can do nothing but flee! Amen.*

To remember:
- Today's decisions are tomorrow's reality.
- An enemy is anyone or anything that feeds your dominant weakness.
- Don't let the Enemy manipulate your emotions to get you off track and off purpose.
- Wherever your life is going, you get there "head" first.

For next time:

Please read part 6, "Prowling Your Neighborhood," before getting back together with your group for session 5. Be on the lookout for signs that your struggle is being played out within your dearest relationships.

SESSION 5

Based on part 6, "Prowling Your Neighborhood" (page 125)

Review:

One of the saddest results of war is the "collateral damage"—the death and injury caused among noncombatants, including women and children. And then there's the tragedy of civil war—brother fighting against brother. Both kinds of tragedies can happen in our battle with our enemy.

Our close relationships—with parents, siblings, spouse, children, good friends, business partners, and so on—are so important to us that it's no wonder they become battlegrounds. We have to keep in mind the realities of human nature: all of us are capable of both good and evil, and all of us have limitations that will cause us to fall short of others' expectations. But still, we can't let anyone, even someone we love dearly, prevent us from doing what God has called us to.

With all this in mind, we must be wise and follow guidelines like these:

- Avoid people who say they want to be our friends but who are really our enemies.
- Watch out for friends who would betray us to our enemies.
- Avoid close association with people who don't see things substantially the way we do.
- Be slow and cautious about admitting people into intimacy with us.
- Recognize that only a few relationships are meant to be permanent; most are just for a season.
- Protect our children—because the Enemy would love to snuff out their potential.

Key scripture:

"A man's enemies will be those of his own household" (Matthew 10:36).

Questions:

1. *How have the members of your family, or others close to you, suffered as a result of your struggle with an enemy?*

2. The author points out that some conflict is simply the result of unrealistic expectations—thinking that others can be better than, or different than, they are. *Can you give an example to illustrate this from your own life?*

3. *Have you ever had a loved one or good friend try to prevent you from fulfilling God's plan for your life? If so, describe it. What did you learn about overcoming the obstacle without rejecting the person?*

4. Ron describes "wolves in sheep's clothing" (people who seem to be friends but are really enemies) and "Judases" (people who are truly your friends but who nevertheless are capable of selling you out to your enemies). *Describe a run-in you've had with one or both of these dangerous types of people. How can we recognize a "wolf" or a "Judas" before such a person does us harm?*

5. Ron says, "I observe it every day: people give sensitive things away to others who haven't yet earned it." *What trouble have you gotten into by letting someone get too close to you too fast?*

6. In this part, Ron repeats an illustration by T. D. Jakes: Some people are like buildings—they're permanent parts of our lives. Others are like scaffolding—they help us in building who we are but aren't meant to remain in our lives forever. *Give an example of someone God has assigned to you for your lifetime. Then give an example of someone who has entered your life only for a season. Why is it important to discern the difference between the two types of relationships?*

7. The author quotes 1 Peter 5:8 (NLT): "Stay alert! Watch out for your great enemy, the devil. He prowls around like a roaring lion, looking for someone to devour." *What can you do to stand between this ravenous predator and your children or other loved ones?*

Prayer:

Father, give us discerning minds about our relationships. Help us to love and accept those You have put into our lives, while excluding those You tell us don't belong in our lives. May we learn to cooperate with our loved ones so that they help us in fulfilling our purpose and we help them in fulfilling theirs. Of all our relationships, though, Lord, we declare that our relationship with You will always be number one! In Jesus's name, amen.

To remember:
- Covenant relationships were meant for you to work together against whatever enemy is attacking that covenant.
- Conflict is the gap between expectations and reality.
- Your inability to discern the role of certain relationships in your life will create enemies.

For next time:
Please read part 7, "How to Fight to Win," before getting back together with your group for session 6. In your mind, review what you've been doing to defeat your enemy.

SESSION 6

Based on part 7, "How to Fight to Win" (page 151)

Review:
Part 7 gives tips to help you win your battle. No one who's facing an enemy should forget this advice:
- Hold on to a quiet, humble faith in what God has told you.
- Trust in God's grace and mercy. His mercy means you won't have to face more than you can handle. His grace means He will give you everything you need to be victorious.
- Pick your battles, so that you don't waste your effort in fruitless fighting.
- Never give up.
- Use your enemy as a stepstool to rise to the next level.
- Seek out wise advice from mentors.
- Don't bother answering your critics.
- Stay in a godly environment so that you fight your enemy on a battlefield of your choosing, not his.
- Be willing to leave where you're at to arrive where God wants to take you.

- Realize that it's ultimately the Lord's battle, not yours.
- Focus on how big God is, not how big your enemy is.
- Follow the lead of the Holy Spirit inside you.

Key scripture:

"Do not be afraid nor dismayed because of this great multitude, for the battle is not yours, but God's" (2 Chronicles 20:15).

Questions:

1. Ron says that Peter did not walk on water; he walked on Jesus's word calling him onto the waves. And likewise we can be a part of miraculous events if we have unwavering trust in God's word to us. *How is your faith in God holding up under the attacks of your enemy? What could strengthen your faith?*

2. God's grace—one of the nukes in your arsenal—ensures that He will give you what you need to be victorious. *What should you be asking God for in prayer to help you in your battle?*

3. Ron suggests two questions to ask when you are trying to decide whether to get into a battle or not. (1) Are there spoils to be gained through victory in this battle? (2) Does this situation threaten my destiny? *If you can see a potential battle in the offing in your life, answer those two questions about it.*

4. Perhaps the simplest advice Ron gives in the whole book is to keep standing, persevere, and outlast your enemy. *Right now, are you more determined to keep going or more tempted to raise the white flag? What can give you the resolve to hold out until the end?*

5. Ron says, "All of us can ultimately learn life's lessons only two ways: we can learn through an experience or learn through what someone who's wise tells us.... Learning from someone else's experiences, both good and bad, is so much easier than taking the knocks yourself." *What mentors or other advisors do you have available to give you wise guidance?*

6. In a military war, the army that gets to choose the battlefield has a distinct advantage. *What worldly environments would the Enemy like to get you into? What can you do to remain in a godly environment that puts the Enemy at a disadvantage?*

7. Abraham had to *leave* his homeland before he could *receive* the blessing God offered. *What comfort zone is God calling you to leave?*

8. *What does the phrase "the battle is the Lord's" mean to you in your particular struggle?*

Prayer:

> *God, we're coming to understand that, while the stakes in our*
> *battles are high, Your place over our circumstances is higher still.*
> *Give us what we need in the battle—resources from within*
> *ourselves, from allies, and especially from You. We acknowledge*
> *that the battle is Yours, and we call on You to win it! Amen.*

To remember:

- It's your enemy's role to create circumstances around you that challenge the faith inside you.
- An enemy will let you swing away all day, and you accomplish nothing except wearing yourself out.
- To get out from underneath the threat of an enemy, change what you're magnifying.
- The Holy Spirit living inside you will guide you into the things God has for you in your life.

For next time:

Please read part 8, "The Spoils of Victory," before getting back together with your group for session 7.

SESSION 7

Based on part 8, "The Spoils of Victory" (page 183)

Review:

Ron Carpenter's battle with his enemy finally came to an end when the lawsuit against him was settled. His church reaped the spoils of victory because, instead of being destroyed, it went on to a new season of effectiveness. And his family reaped the spoils too as they grew closer together than ever.

If we will handle the conclusion of our battle wisely, we also can make the most of the victory God gives.

A hard-fought battle inevitably leaves scars. But God gives healing. If you've experienced a victory, don't let your guard down, because another attack might be following behind. If you need some healing, get away—because changing your environment can often help in recovery. If you realize that you made some mistakes along the way, trust God to make adjustments and guide you into His plan anyway. If you don't know what to do next, give yourself time to regroup and hear from God. And in the meantime, hang out with other Christians who will let you be honest about what you're going through and help you recover.

Key scripture:

"In all these things we are more than conquerors through Him who loved us" (Romans 8:37).

Questions:

1. *Have you experienced any degree of victory over your enemy yet? If so, describe it. What are the benefits you're seeing for you and your family? for your God-given purpose in life?*

2. After achieving a stunning victory over the pagan priests at Mount Carmel, the prophet Elijah emotionally folded up when a wicked queen threatened him. Ron says that Elijah's example "points to the fact that the aftermath of a victory is a vulnerable time." *How might you be vulnerable to a follow-up attack right now?*

3. *What wounds and scars has your struggle left in your life?*

4. The author advises a change of location to find needed healing. "You may not be able to go away by leaving town," he says, "but in some way, for at least a short period of time—even a few hours—you need to find a way to change your environment so the Holy Spirit can help you see reality and adjust your perspective. And bring needed rest and healing." *How could you put yourself in a different place where you might be more likely to receive healing?*

5. Wise commanders debrief their sides' performance after a battle. *As you review your decisions during your battle, what mistakes do you see that you made?* The author says that, just as a GPS device in a car can recalculate a route after a wrong turn, so God can get us back on course even if we think we have made some disastrous miscalculations. *How do you need God to reset your course in life?*

6. Even though winning a victory over your enemy is a terrific thing, you still might feel some emptiness or aimlessness. *What words would you use to describe your emotional state right now? How can you give yourself a chance to regroup and let your emotional health and energy bounce back?*

7. Jesus said to the man with a withered hand, "Stretch out your hand"—referring to his unhealthy hand, not his healthy one. Likewise, churches and other Christian groups should be places where people can appropriately reveal their wounds and find healing. *What have you appreciated most about how this small group has helped you during your battle with an enemy? What other individuals or groups can you go to for continuing acceptance and encouragement?*

Prayer:

Father, we thank You for the success You have brought and are going to bring. Don't let us allow the spoils of victory to slip through our fingers by responding to our victory in the wrong way. Help us to cement the advantages You bring. Help us to heal, to learn, and to move on to what You have for us next. We know You are not done with us yet. And we know the Enemy is not done with us yet either. Take us from victory to victory and from Christlikeness to greater Christlikeness…and in the end to the ultimate victory in which all Your sons and daughters will share by Your grace. In Jesus's name, amen.

To remember:

- Sometimes a Goliath has to get in your face to bring about needed changes.
- Just because your life is transitioning doesn't mean it's ending.
- Jesus created an atmosphere where weaknesses could be healed.

ACKNOWLEDGMENTS

After over four decades of life with over twenty years in ministry, this first book is long overdue. There are some very special people in my life I need to thank.

To the incredible family of Redemption World Outreach Center in Greenville, South Carolina and around the world, who have been gracious and kind enough to cheer me on and share me with the world...thank you from the bottom of my heart.

I want to thank my mom and dad for the godly heritage and the deep investment they made in my life. You modeled in front of me a godly home, and I'm forever grateful.

To my children: Chase, Chaz, and Chanlin, no matter where God allows me to go in life, you have always been and will always be my greatest accomplishment.

And to my dearest wife, Hope, my ministry partner, my very best friend, outside of Jesus you are the greatest thing that ever happened to me. Thank you for all the sacrifices you have made to be the kind of woman you are. I can't wait for the rest of my life with you.